DECENTRALISED PLANNING AND THE DISTRICT PLANNING COMMITTEES

S. N. Singh

KALPAZ

ISBN: 978-93-5128-064-4
Price: ₹ 425

First Published, 2014

Published by

Kalpaz Publications
C-30, Satyawati Nagar,
Delhi-110052
Ph. : 9212142040
E-mail: kalpaz@hotmail.com

Laser Typesetting : Gyan Prints (AB-II), Delhi
Printed at : G. Print Process, Delhi

Cataloging in Publication Data—DK
Courtesy: D.K. Agencies (P) Ltd.
<docinfo@dkagencies.com>

Singh, S. N.
Decentralised planning and the district planning committees / S.N. Singh.
p. cm.
Includes bibliographical references and index.
ISBN 9789351280644

1. Decentralization in government—India. 2. Regional planning—India. 3. Rural development projects—India. I. Title.

DDC 351.54 23

Contents

Preface

India opted for a planned approach to achieve progress and development after it attained its independence. Amongst the various approaches and models of development, the country opted for decentralised planning model from the initial years of planning. However, not much progress could be achieved in actually adopting the decentralised planning process. We do find efforts through the Five Year Plan as well as the Planning Commission appointing committees to go into the problem of formally accepting the decentralised planning model for development. It took considerable time and effort before decentralised planning was finally accepted.

The decentralised planning through District Planning Committees (DPC) became a reality through the Constitution reforms of early nineties, where a provision for the forming of District Planning Committee was incorporated in the Constitution itself. Consequent upon this Constitutional provision, the States across the country took steps of formally constitute District Planning Committees in their States. Some States did constitute the DPC while others took time and the process got delayed. After the intervention of the Planning Commission most of the States constituted the DPC. The plan preparation and consolidation at the district level began once these DPCs were constituted: The DPCs, thus, have a definite role in the decentralised planning as it is through these the planning has to be operationalised.

The present book is based on the study which has gone into the question of decentralised planning process making an attempt to assess as to how far the same has been effective in achieving the desired goals. It has examined the composition of the DPCs along with the functions performed by these bodies over the years. The observation and the opinions are based on the analysis of data received through primary as well as secondary sources. We have, identified the problem areas in the composition and consolidation of district plan by the DPCs and have provided suggestions to counter the problems. It is hoped that the book would be able to address the issues in this important sector of our development.

S. N. Singh

1

Introduction

After independence India began its journey for reconstruction and growth with a planned approach. In order to give shape to these goals in reality, a new organisation in the name of National Planning Commission was formed through a Cabinet Resolution of the government of India in the year 1950. India's planning experiment started with a complete centralised process. The objectives, goals, strategies and priorities were set out at the national level by the Planning Commission, the apex body created for the purpose. Centralised planning was considered essential to control and augment national economy and to gear-up national development in India after her emergence from the long period of colonial exploitation. The process thus continued to be characterised grossly by a "top down", bureaucratic-technocratic approach rather than a grassroots,—participative one[1]. This is seen as the initial approach towards planning in India.

A debate on the strategies for proper development in the country soon started along with the planning process. The Second Five Year Plan initiated the concept of "planning from below" which remained in focus in subsequent Plans. A debate about decentralised planning can be seen in contemporary literatures on planning in India. It was argued that decentralised planning or planning from below helps the planners to decide the objectives and priorities in the sight of specific requirements of a locality vis-à-vis the availability of resources[2].

There is no denying the fact that a well-organised planning body at the grassroots level is capable of comprehending the situation, so as to identify specifically the logjam standing on the way of growth and development.

There could be more than a few objectives of planning, but one of the basic objectives of planning is to balance the disparities among different parts of the country. It is particularly true for India which witnesses imbalances of various kinds. The regional and economical influence, inference the social imbalance and the vice-versa. Usually, the planners adopted both the short-term and long-term policies from time to time with a view to reducing the uneven space of development among the region and to the paucity of natural resources. Such a belief is untenable in modern times since it is well-known fact now that many of the poor regions are otherwise rich in resources, both natural and human. Hence, the planners would have to find ways and means to reduce the inter-regional disparities and to break the vicious circle of poverty and backwardness with determined and deliberate choice of suitable measures. It has also been advocated that decentralised planning through its thrust on area specific development program within a multi-level framework may help to solve the problem of regional imbalances and intra-regional differences[3]. A case for decentralised planning is made out to counter the shortcomings of macro-level planning.

Moreover, decentralised planning is also considered necessary to integrate and coordinate the activities and progress undertaken by various department of the government. It has been observed that under the centralised planning system the usual practice is that the district officials, even when district planning is undertaken, continue to compile information and prepare only departmental proposals in isolation with little appreciation of the comprehensive nature of planning and the need for proper integration and co-ordination of sectoral or departmental plans. Most of the projects of the government have failed in the past due to lack of the co-ordination and interlinking. The execution of programmes become difficult when there exist multiple agencies for the same purpose including Panchayati Raj bodies and others. In such a situation, district planning is considered to be an effective instrument in dovetailing the various resources for different schemes and projects in an integrated way[4]. This is considered to be a more rationalistic way.

It may be worth recollecting that repeated efforts starting from the days of Community Development in the 1950s, to the days of the Pilot Research Project in Growth Centres during the Fourth Five Year Plan period, early efforts at planning through the panchayat bodies, the issuing of guidelines for District Planning by the Planning Commission in 1969 and on through the 1970, including talk of Block Level Planning following the Dantwala Committee Report of 1978, and culminating in the Hanumantha Rao report on District Planning of 1984, all show that despite the failure of district or regional planning to take off in India, the need for such decentralised planning has been repeatedly felt and such a need is still felt by most is evidenced from the recent debate on decentralised planning, initiated by the former Prime Minister which evoked mixed response about the detailed modalities and motivations. But no one has questioned the need for decentralised planning and even after the recent change of government at the national level decentralised planning has been re-emphasised[5]. Such decentralised planning is being considered useful both from the view point of greater efficiency in resource mobilisation and its allocation, as well as from the view point of grassroots democracy and greater power to people.

It may be worth nothing here that the Hanumantha Rao Report as well as the F.A.O.'s Economic and Social Development Paper 52 have used almost identical language about the stages through which the decentralised planning process has to move. It proposed a three-stage process to achieve 'full' decentralisation. Under the stage I, it identified the pre-requisite for the decentralised planning which included various steps needed for the purpose. The Stage II called for 'limited' decentralisation. Under this stage, it was expected to bring limited sectors activity, e.g. Minimum Needs Program, agriculture and allied activities within the purview of planning at the district level. It also included streamlining of the procedure and for dovetailing district plan into the State Plan. Under the third, i.e., Stage III full or final decentralise is the goal. It included steps to improve and strengthen local government institutions which were supposed to be the new agency through which decentralisation was to be achieved. It also included steps to encourage and provide for high-level of popular participation. It may, however, be noted that not much ice could be cut and his recommendation remained of academic interest. But the issue of decentralised planning remained in focus and subsequent developments would show the steps taken in this direction.

Decentralised Planning Through Five Year Plan

Once India chooses for planned development, district planning or the decentralised planning became an integral part of the planning strategy. Although the Fifth Five Year Plan emphasised the importance of the decentralised planning, nothing substantial was done to put the process into practice. In order to reduce poverty in rural India and ensure people's participation in the development program, Community Development Programme was launched in 1952 by creating 55 development Blocks throughout the country which increased to 1075 at the end of the First Five Year Plan[6].

The Community Development Program was supposed to be a method of rural development based on people's participation which sought to initiate the process of democratic decentralisation for the transformation of the social and economic life of the villages in a co-ordinated and planned way. The First Five Year Plan accepted the principle of democratic planning in which people's co-operation was solicited in the implementation of the plan programs.

These considerations were taken into consideration during the formulation of Second Five Year Plan. In spite of the contradiction in the ideology of the Second Five Year Plan, it emphasised the need for inclusion of local varieties into national and state plans. The Second Five Year Plan stressed the need for creating effective administration and developmental institutions at the base level for decentralised planning and rural development: unless there is a comprehensive village planning which takes into account the need of the entire community; weaker sections like tenants, cultivators, landless workers and village artisans may not benefit sufficiently from assistance provided by the Government. Secondly, rural progress depends entirely upon the existence of an active organisation in the villages which can approach each family and bring all people including the weaker sections of the community into production and other programmes to be carried out with the help of administration[7].

The Second Five Year Plan emphasised the need for district planning including the planning for the blocks, and groups of villages and municipal areas. The need for creating a well-organised structure of administration at district level and below was being felt. The practice followed hitherto in planning and development remained almost the same during this period although the Second Five Year Plan discussed the concept and the scope of decentralised horizontal plans in great details[8].

During the initial period of Second Five Year Plan, an important event took place having a far-reaching implication in the fields of decentralisation in administration and development planning. The event was the appointment of Balwantrai Mehta Study Team to evaluate the plan projects under the Community Development Programme. The recommendation of the Committee led to the genesis of Panchayati Raj Institution. The Committee recommended for a three-tier structure of Panchayati Raj institutions. The Committee stressed the need for planning rural development administration fairly at the hands of local representatives of people to ensure people's participation in the development works at the local level.

The introduction of the Panchayati Raj system by the end of the Second Five Year Plan added a new dimension to the concept of development administration. This plan laid much emphasis on district development administration especially on the models on which District Development Councils were proposed to be built up in future. Then, the district development administration was considered as an agency of change towards a new social order... to respond to the needs and aspirations of the people[9]. The Third Five Year Plan attached considerable importance to decentralised planning and identified district level programmes similar on the lines contained in the Second Five Year Plan. During the Third Plan, attempts were made to provide state plans taking the district plan into account.

It is worth noting that the real breakthrough in the sphere of planning process was made during the Fourth Five Year Plan period where some concrete steps were taken by the Planning Commission to decentralise the planning system. Credit for this shift in outlook goes primarily to D.R. Gadgil, the then Deputy Chairman of the Planning Commission, who popularised the concept of district plan. Prior to the launching of the Fourth Five Year Plan, India's planning was highly centralised in both concept and conduct[10]. In spite of the prevalent practice in the matter of plan formulation, there was little difference among the politicians and planners on the desirability and need for changing the existing system of centralised and sectoral planning. But little thought was given to concretise the idea of decentralised planning.

It was in 1969, that the Planning Commission finally decided to settle down at the district level and recommended district as the unit of both plan formulation and execution and issued guidelines for the formulation of District Plan. The Commission on its part advised the States to adopt district as the unit of planning below the State level and to put emphasis on the integration of the plan of local self-government bodies, Panchayati Raj Institution, Co-operative organisations and government departments. The guidelines also recommended continuous consultation not only after the preparation of plan but also before and during the formulation of plans. However, in practice these consultation remained only on paper and not much could be achieved so far as the actual decentralisation in the planning process is concerned.

Looking at the planning process, it could well be observed that during the first two plans there was no specific program, but only statements and declaration regarding regional planning and development. Only the Third Five Year Plan made some headway in this direction. However, it was the Fourth Five Year Plan which spelt out for the first time concrete steps in the direction of multi-level planning with district as the main focus in the process. Subsequently, the concept of decentralised district planning became a development strategy which necessitated the creation of an infrastructure and an effective change in the attitude of bureaucrats and politicians for the success of the decentralised planning. Both, the Fourth and Fifth Five Year Plans were directed towards decentralisation taking district and the block and the micro-levels of planning to speed up the work of planned rural development. An attempt was made for the first time to treat the villages as the lowest unit of decentralised planning by adopting the scheme *'Antyodaya'* in 1977 in order to bring about the integrated development of the village as a whole[11]. The program like 'Food for work' was also launched to combat poverty through the decentralised planning process.

Far-reaching changes were witnessed in the national political arena when Janata Party government was formed in 1977. The establishment of Janata Party Government paved the way for real experiments in decentralisation in the system of both administration and planning. Special mention may be made about two important committees viz., the Working Group on Block Level Planning, headed by M.L. Dantewala and the Committee on Panchayati Raj popularly known as Ashok Mehta Committee in 1977. Both these Committees made important recommendations about decentralised planning in the country. As a matter of fact, the national debate on decentralisation in planning was revived after the submission of these two Reports. But owing to changes in political scenario at the national level with Congress coming back to power much development could not be achieved on the recommendation of these two Committees.

However, the Sixth Five Year Plan sought to accommodate the recommendations of these Committees and adopted the strategy to strengthen the process of decentralisation[12]. Moreover, the Planning Commission appointed a Working Group on District Planning in 1982 under the Chairmanship of C.H. Hanumantha Rao and the recommendations of this group formed the basis for evolving the district planning and the approach was outlined in the Seventh Plan. The Seventh Five Year Plan incorporated the main ideas outlined in the recommendation of the Working Group and stated to pursue 'the decentralised of planning process' for development. It was also realised that the planning activities at the district level would vest in single district planning body which would determine the strategies and priorities and allocates funds for various departments taking into account the planning and other capabilities available at the grassroots level[13]. The idea of decentralised planning got a further fillip in the recommendation of the Commission on Centre-State Relations popularly known as Sarkaria Commission and the Committee to Review the Existing Administrative Arrangements for Rural Development and Poverty Alleviation (RAARD), headed by G.K.V. Rao.

The G.K.V. Rao Committee (CAARD) while dealing with the issue of decentralised planning endorsed the major recommendations of the Working Group on District Planning in respect of setting up district planning bodies and the decentralisation and devolution of administrative and financial powers[14]. But the findings of the CAARD were somewhat different from those of the Working Group report on district planning as the CAARD emphasised the representative leadership of the Panchayati Raj Institutions at different levels[15]. Highlighting the planning operation as a single holistic one, the Committee, in broad agreement with the approach to decentralisation, indicated by the Working Group, suggested the total accommodation of local needs and aspirations in the district plan. The Committee stressed the need for establishing a sound planning and implementing machinery for effective integration and co-ordination of all the rural development activities under the 'umbrella of district planning'[16]. It also recommended the rationalisation in the activities of different institutions of development activities at the district level under the effective leadership of democratic bodies of local governance[17]. These recommendations together with those of the two Working Groups provided the ideological and operational foundation of district planning in India.

The Eighth Five Year Plan stressed the role of the government to make possible the process of people's participation through the creation of necessary institutional infrastructure particularly in the rural areas. A review of the planning process provides enough indication that the Eighth Plan itself was involved in an experiment in district planning though the importance of decentralisation was widely established. Decentralised planning and the district planning have consistently received attention of the planners, but in reality we find a number of shortcomings because of which decentralised planning could not properly take shape.

Constitutional Amendments and Decentralised Planning

We have briefly noted the developments that have taken place over the years in the sphere of decentralised planning. In spite of the constant efforts not much real progress could be made in making the decentralised planning effective. Observers feel that the neglected state of affairs in the process of decentralised planning, the overall progress in effective decentralisation through Panchayati Raj was not at all satisfactory. There was a growing realisation that the ineffectiveness and non-functioning of rural local self-governing bodies were the result of the absence of constitutional recognition to the Panchayati Raj Institution, articulated by Ashok Mehta Committee gained ground in the reports of the Thungon Committee which recommended constitutional status for these bodies[18]. Even earlier attempts have been made by various groups and forums for granting constitutional status to local government bodies, both rural and urban. It was continuously been improved that these self-governing bodies are suffering on various counts at the hands of State government and therefore, there is a need to grant them a constitutional status to improve upon their performance.

The continuous demand and the pressure ultimately bore fruits. The 73rd and 74th Constitutional Amendment Act (1992) is considered as *middle stone* in the field of decentralisation in administration and planning. The Amendment seeks to initiate a genuine process of decentralised planning with the total involvement of local self-governing institutions together with the District Planning Committee and Metropolitan Planning Committee[19]. These twin amendments contain larger implications for decentralised planning process since the attempt to evaluate the status of the panchayats and the municipalities as effective institutions of self-governance by making the Panchayati Raj, District Planning Committee, and the Metropolitan Planning Committee as necessary parts of the basic structure of the Constitution itself. The amendments also seek to ensure periodical elections and assign active and enhanced role to them in the planning process. Thus, the amendments may be considered as the culmination of the long debate that was revived in the aftermath of Ashok Mehta and Dantewala Committee reports.

It can now be seen that the 73rd and 74th Constitutional Amendments have paved the way for multi-level planning in India. The constitutional stipulation for the establishment of District Planning Committee at the district level and the Gram Sabha at the village level can be seen as the structural means for devolution of decision-making power from the Centre to the grassroots level together with other constitutional provision giving new meaning and content to multi-level decision-making process of which Panchayati and District Planning Committees have become institutions of self-governance throughout the country. The 73rd Constitutional Amendment Act provides for devolution of powers and responsibilities upon the panchayats at the appropriate levels for preparation of plans for economic development and social justice[20]. An elaborate list of 29 items has been included in the Eleventh Schedule which adds a new dimension to the devolution of power outlined in the 73rd Amendment. Thus, the Panchayati Raj Institutions in collaboration with District Planning Committee have now become Constitutional institutions for planning and development below the state level.

In the backdrop of above, we find that the Nineth Five Year Plan gave due emphasis on decentralised district planning but the final outcome of the effort remained debatable. But nonetheless the Ninth Plan stressed that the decentralised planning in India has now become a reality. Looking at the initial concept of decentralised planning starting from the First Five Year Plan, it has taken more than four decades to become a reality. In the preceding pages we have tried to briefly cover the journey through various Five Year Plans.

Some Recent Initiatives

After giving a brief overview of the state of decentralised planning during different plans period, let us now briefly focus upon the initiatives taken in the recent past. In this context, it may be noted that the Ministry of Panchayati Raj, Government of India, convened a number of Round Table meetings. The Second Round Table meeting regarding decentralised planning made a number of recommendations. Some of those recommendations were as follows (Approach Paper, Eleventh Five Year Plan 2007):

- District Planning Committee ought to be constituted in every state by the end of the financial year 2004-05 in accordance with the procedure laid down in Article 243. ZD (2).
- All States ought to make provisions by law, utilising the functions and procedure by D.P.Cs.
- District Planning ought to take into account the area's resources endowment, people's felt needs and their relative absorption capacity.
- Each level of panchayats and municipalities ought to prepare perspective Five Year Plan and Annual Plan as provided in the Constitution, which could be consolidated by the D.P.C.
- The State must specify institution, organisations and individuals to assist panchayats, municipalities and D.P.Cs in preparing plans in accordance with Article 243ZD (3)(b).
- State must indicate extent and type of available resources to each Panchayat Level and municipalities as per Article 243ZD in order to facilitate planning.
- Central Government could consider establishing a mechanism to pool all Central Government Finance Commission's resources, for channelising them to panchayats.
- State must strengthen the finances of the PRIs so that planning at the District and Sub-district level is based on an indication of the available resources.

In view of these recommendations, the Planning Commission wrote to the State Governments to consider several points, raised before making proposals in the forthcoming Eleventh Five Year Plan. It can, thus, be argued that the Government of India as well as the State Government have taken steps to strengthen the decentralised planning structure. In making the constitution of the District Planning Committees a constitutional exercise can be said to be a step forward toward that effort. It can further be observed that on the part of the Government of India we have already noted the efforts that have gone into making decentralised planning finally takes shape in the country. However, it would still remain with the State Governments to take positive steps in the direction of making decentralised planning a success. The Expert Group of Government of India, Ministry of Panchayati Raj in its observation have made a number of critical comments and observation. A cursory glance at the Report would show that there are a number of States which still have to take steps in the direction of making statutory provision for the creation of District Planning Committee and also take follow up action of constituting the same.

The scenario regarding decentralised planning through District planning Committee rose in despite the direction from the Government of India in this regard. Different states were at different stages with regard to constituting and making the District Planning Committee functional. It remained a matter of anxiety to the effectiveness or otherwise of the District Planning Committee is concerned. It called for an objective assessment to understand the real situation.

The Need and Importance of the Study

Ever since, India decided on for planning as a strategy for achieving growth and development, decentralised planning remained an important component of that effort. It is more than five decades since the concept has been in operation. It received added impetus through the 73rd and 74th Constitutional Amendment Act, 1992. Decentralised planning was accorded a constitutional status and consequent upon this a hope has arisen regarding the effectiveness of decentralised planning through the District Planning Committees. In pursuance of these Acts, several States have made statutory provision for constituting the District Planning Committee. It is about two decades since the Central Act was passed. It is reasonable to have an objective evaluation as to how the scheme has fared. It is worthwhile having a rational assessment of the status of decentralised planning in the country as to how far it has been able to achieve the desired objectives. A need for this kind of study is generally felt in view of the importance of decentralised planning for an effective and a realistic planned development. In view of its importance for general societal development, the present study was proposed with the following as its main objective:

- To study the organisation and structure of decentralised planning structure with focus on District Planning Committees.

- To examine this methods and procedure of decentralised planning with particular reference to District Planning Committee.
- To assess the effectiveness of decentralised planning in achieving the goal and targets set forth for development.
- To identify the difference in development perspective in two areas of with and without a District Planning Committee.
- To study specifically the role of District Planning Committee in decentralised planning.
- To identify the problem areas in decentralised planning.
- To suggest changes in the present organisation and process of decentralised planning in case needed to better development administration.

Scope and Methodology

So far as the scope of the study is concerned, it had an all India perspective. Decentralised planning has been accepted as an important strategy for rural development; the overall coverage therefore, has been the entire country. Since decentralised planning is under the State list of subjects of the Constitution, variations of various natures are bound to be there despite statutory provision. In order to have a detailed analysis of the organisation and the process connected with decentralised planning, two states namely, Andhra Pradesh from south and Uttar Pradesh from north were selected. The detailed primary as well as secondary sources of data have specially been collected from these selected states.

After choosing these two states, further two districts from each of the selected states were picked for the collection of data from the field. The selected districts were as under:

1. Andhra Pradesh
   1. Rangareddy
   2. Chittoor
2. Uttar Pradesh
   1. Gorakhpur
   2. Bareilly

The study, bases itself from the data collected from the states of Andhra Pradesh and Uttar Pradesh, so far as the involvement of the state administration is concerned. Further data about the District Planning Committee is largely collected from the selected districts themselves, apart from the supportive data picked from th secondary sources. The study has, therefore made use of both the sources of data in forming opinion. For the primary sources, two different sets of questionnaire, one for the officials and the other for non-official, were designed and administered on the selected respondents (A copy of the questionnaire is annexed with the report as Annexure I). The secondary sources of data included information collected from relevant books, reports, journals and other published material connected with the subject. This study also made use of observation as a research tool.

Data so collected was processed through computer and tables were prepared for analysis. The final report thus, bases itself on these data and information.

References

1. Jana, Anil Kumar, Administering District Plans in India, Concept Publishing Company, New Delhi, 2004, p. 25.
2. Misra R.P. and Sunderan K.V., 1988, in Mooris Raja (Ed.), Regional Development, New Delhi, Heritage Publication, p. 68.
3. Sixth Five Year Plan, Govt. of India, New Delhi, 1980, p. 93.
4. Report of the Working Group on District Planning 1984, Govt. of India, New Delhi, p. 56.
5. Hooja, Rakesh and Mathur, P.C. (Ed.) District and Decentralised Planning, Rawat Publication, Jaipur, 1991, pp. 15-16.
6. First Five Year Plan, 1952, Govt. of India, New Delhi, p. 140.
7. The Second Five Year Plan, Govt. of India, New Delhi, 1956.
8. Report of the Working Group on District Planning, 1984, p. 21.
9. The Second Five Year Plan, *op. cit.* p. 164.
10. Jara, Anil Kumar, *op. cit.* p. 40.
11. Report of the Department of Rural Development, 1978-79, Govt. of India, New Delhi, pp. 15-19.
12. Sixth Five Year Plan, 1980, Govt. of India, New Delhi, p. 176.
13. Report of the Working Group on District Planning, 1985, *op. cit.* p. 23.
14. Report of the CAARD, 1985, p. 30, para 4. 21.
15. *Ibid.,* p. 45, para (5) 6.25 and 6.26.
16. *Ibid.,* pp. 27-28, para 4.11.
17. *Ibid.,* para 4.21.
18. *Note:* A Sub-Committee of the Consultative Committees of Parliament was appointed under the Chairmanship of P.K. Thungon in 1988, which recommended that Panchayati Raj Institution should be constitutionally recognised.
19. Constitution of Indian Article 243 ZD.
20. The Constitution of India, Article 243G.

2

Profile of the Universe

For the purpose of detailed data collection two States of the Indian Union, namely Andhra Pradesh and Uttar Pradesh were selected. We now present a brief profile of the selected State.

(A) ANDHRA PRADESH

Andhra Pradesh is the fifth largest State in India and it forms the major link between the north and the south of India. It is the biggest and most populous State in the South of India. It falls into a drought zone in some years due to the South-West monsoon rain that arrives late.

It is bounded by Madhya Pradesh, Chhattisgarh and Orissa in the North, the Bay of Bengal in the East, Tamil Nadu and Karnataka in the South and Maharashtra in the West.

Area

Andhra Pradesh lies between 12°41' and 22° N latitude and 77° and 840 40 E Longitudes. It is spread over an area of 275,068 sq. km.

Climate

Andhra Pradesh receives rainfall from the South-West monsoon as well as the North-East monsoon. The first rainfall begins in the second week of June, and it lasts till September while the second rainfall occurs in October-November.

The State's coastal areas receive heavy rains during the North-East monsoon and are also subject to cyclonic conditions which cause enormous damage to residential accommodation, and to standing crops. The rainfall decreases from north to south. The Nizamabad district in Telangana receives about 87.5 cm. of rain while Anantpur in Rayalaseema receives only 31 cm.

The State has a really hot summer but after the rain begins in the middle of June, there is a decline in the heat when humidity takes over. There is a mild winter in December but the temperature does not go down below 16°C. While the South-West monsoon is comparatively heavy in the northern parts of the State, the North-East monsoon brings more rain to the southern areas like Rayalaseema. The hot season causes the mercury to rise to worrying proportions in the month of April and May, when it could shoot up to 40 degrees and more.

Physiography

The three main geomorphic provinces of Andhra Pradesh are:

1. The coastal plains, blessed with excellent weather and rich alluvial plains.
2. The eastern ghats which consist of exotic forest and rivers running through rocky hills.
3. Coal beds, geneses, granites and basaltic lava that constitute the peninsular plateau.

Soils

The state has red, black alluvial lateric and coastal sandy soil, with shale and limestone landscapes also present.

Hills

The state is dotted with hill ranges from the north to the south, running erratically down the middle of the country dividing it into western and eastern coastal Andhra. These hills form integral geographical entities of Andhra life and history.

In the north, there are Simhachalam and Annavaram hills, in the middle country there are one, the Sri Sailam hill ranges and in the south, Tirumalai/Tirupati hills.

Rivers

The State has two great rivers, Godavari and Krishna which spring from the Western Ghats in Maharashtra and flow eastward and joins the Bay of Bengal. Besides these two big rivers there are the Tungabhadra, the Pennar and many other small rivers and rivulets. Pennar originates in the Karnataka plateau.

Population Characteristics

The total population of Andhra Pradesh as of 1st March 2001, stood at 75,727,541 as per the provisional results of the census of India 2001. Males constituted 38,286,811 of the population while females constituted 37,440,730 of the population. The sex ratio (females per thousand males) stood at 978. Andhra Pradesh is the 5th largest state in India, both in terms of area and population.

Characteristics of People

Sanskrit writings from the 7th century B.C. describe the Andhra people as Aryans from the North who migrated south of the Vindhya range and mixed with Dravidians. They are mentioned again at the time of the death of the Great Mauryan King Ashoka in 232 B.C. This date has been held to be the beginning of the Andhra historical record. Various dynasties have ruled the area, including the Andhra (or Satvahana), Shakas, Ikshvakus, eastern Chalukyas Vijai Nagar, the Qutb Shahis, and the Nizams (princes) of Hyderabad.

During the 17th Century, the British acquired from the Nizams first the coastal area (the province of Madras) and then the inland region of what is now Andhra Pradesh. Andhras were at the forefront of Indian nationalism in the late 19th and early 20th centuries. Their demands for a separate state for Telugu speakers led to the formation of Andhra Pradesh in 1953 from parts of Madras and Hyderabad states; this led the way for the formation of language-based states throughout India in 1957.

Economy

Agriculture has been the chief source of income for the state's economy. Two important rivers of India, Godavari and Krishna flow through the state. Rice, tobacco, cotton, mirchi and sugarcane are the important crops grown here. The state has also started making some interesting strides in the fields of information technology and bio-technology.

Urban/Rural Distribution of Population

With about 27 per cent of the population living in urban areas, the level of urbanisation in the state is almost on par with the national average. The living standards of the rural people overall remain low, as most of them live under conditions of agrarian overpopulation and limited opportunities for productive work.

Workforce Distribution

The data on workforce distribution indicates a high magnitude of dependency on agriculture. Nearly 80 per cent of the total workers in the state are still engaged in agriculture (cultivators and agricultural labourers put together). The proportion of agricultural labourers in Andhra Pradesh is the highest among all the states in India.

Religious Identities

Andhra Pradesh is a mosaic of different faiths. Buddhism which was a major religion till the early medieval period has become virtually non-existent today. The Hindus including SC, ST constitute 89 per cent of the total population. Muslims are located largely in certain districts and towns, Christians constitute 1.8 per cent in the state. Jains, Buddhists and Sikhs constitute 0.4, 0.3 and 0.3 per cent respectively.

The Caste Structure

Among the Dwijas (twice-born castes) the Brahmins constitute about two to three per cent of the states' population. They are still in large numbers in the bureaucracy, mass-media, academic institutions and other vital professions, such as law, scientific research, medicine and management.

The Vysas, known as Komatis in the state, constitute another two to three per cent. Engaged in the traditional occupation of trade, Komatis are omnipresent in the state. They carry on most of the trades, textiles, grains, banking, money-lending, grocery, shop-keeping, pawn broking etc.

Rajus, who claim Kshatriyas status, are mostly confined to the north and central coastal regions, may constitute about one per cent.

The non-Brahmin caste groups such as the Reddis, Kammas, Kapus and Velamas, whose main occupation has been cultivation, are the most important social groups in the state, in terms of numerical strength, land control and access to political power.

The Scheduled Caste and the Scheduled Tribes

Andhra Pradesh is one of the major states with a large concentration of the Scheduled Castes (SCs) with about eight per cent of the total SC population of the country.

There are about 33 tribes, forming about seven per cent of the population of the state.

Backward Castes

Various caste groups, which are known by the names of traditional hereditary occupations, mainly artisan and service occupations, constitute a large proportion of the population in Andhra society, known as backward caste.

The second Andhra Pradesh backward classes commission (1982) estimated that OBC constitute 44 per cent of the state's population.

Struggle for the State

The Andhras were struggling for the formation of a separate Andhra province since the period of British, but could not succeed. When India attained independence, Andhras hoped that their long-cherished desire would be realised soon, but in spite of strenuons effort it remained as a dream itself.

The creation of Andhra Pradesh: On the 1st October, 1953, Andhra state came into existence. It consisted of the districts of Srikakulam, Visakhapatanam, East Godavari, West Godavari, Krishna, Guntur, Nellore, Chittoor, Cuddapah, Anantpur and Kurnool and the Taluks of Rayadury, Adeni and Alur of the Bellary district.

Education

The numbers of recognised education institutions include 16 universities, institutions deemed to be universities five, degree colleges total number is 1402.

A conscious effort is being made to bring symbiosis between the Universities and the industries who happen to be the end users of this skilled manpower.

Micro Planning Community Participation

Micro planning is an instrument for mobilising communities, assessing their contextual needs, improving access and facilitating retention and participation in schools. It has two crucial elements, village or block-based planning and school-based planning.

Transport and Communication

Andhra Pradesh has excellent rail, road and air connections to various parts of the country.

An expansive 1,45,000 km network of roads is on the anvil. 1400 km of major highways is presently being upgraded with aid from the World Bank.

Andhra Pradesh has over 5,000 km of rail lines with one-third of the country's rail cargo passing through the Vijayawada rail terminal.

Eleven ports are spread along the 972 km coast line. Hyderabad houses a fully self-contained inland container freight depot and air cargo complex.

Communication Development

Every district headquarter would be connected by a two MB link. An open-door policy welcomes investment in the manufacture of switching systems, pagers, connectors, various types of cables, transmission equipment and terminals like cordless phones, pay phones, fax machines and modems.

Andhra Pradesh has the largest number of telephone exchanges in the country. Modern communication facilities like cellular and pager services with various networks to choose from are available.

Satellite Communication Centre

The Government of Andhra Pradesh in collaboration with Indian Space Research Organisation (ISRO) intends to create a satellite-based network infrastructure for providing connectivity throughout the state including remote areas. The satellite-based communication network is to be utilised in the following areas:

1. Distance Education,
2. Tele medicine,
3. Agricultural Extension,
4. Human Resource Development,
5. E-governance,
6. Awareness building among self-help groups.

Language and Literature

The main languages spoken in Andhra Pradesh are Telugu, Urdu, Hindi, Banjara and English followed by Tamil, Kannada, Marathi and Oriya. Telugu is the principal and official language of the state. Being a mellifluous language, it is called by its admirers as the "Italian of the east". Its vocabulary is very much influenced by Sanskrit. Until the advent of the printing press and the school system of education, Telugu was broadly used in four areas:

1. Inscriptions,
2. Poetry,
3. Folk literature,
4. Common speech (social and perhaps official).

Medical Facilities

As per the 2001 census, there are 3133 hospitals and 134 dispensaries in Andhra Pradesh. In 1989, a proposal was made that a school health project be established in Andhra Pradesh assisted by the British Overseas Development Administration (ODA) by aid of 6.7 million pounds. The project aimed to develop the state's existing school health programme which included regular medical inspections and treatment but which was hampered due to lack of personnel.

Industry

In 1999-2000, there were 13164 factories in Andhra Pradesh. In 2001-2002, there were 6218 public sector companies and 31081 private sector companies, the total being 37299 companies in Andhra Pradesh.

Transition of Economy

Andhra Pradesh has embarked upon a vigorous effort to create economic growth. From a predominantly agro-based economy, it is transforming itself to a knowledge-focussed economy. It has taken many initiatives in this context, such as economic and regulatory reforms, policy measures to attract private investment, focus on key-growth sectors and providing the necessary government support to nurture private sector initiatives.

Info-tech Industry

Information Technology is increasingly permeating every facet of human endeavour and has radically transformed the way societies work, play, gather and access knowledge and govern themselves.

Bio-tech Industry

Traditional forms of Indian medicine such as Ayurveda, Unani and Siddha are practiced widely in the state.

Natural Wealth

Forest: Twenty-three per cent of Andhra Pradesh is covered with forests and has a diverse and exotic flora and fauna.

Rivers: Constitute a vital element of the consciousness and way of life of the people in the riverine areas. The anicuts across the

Godavari, the Krishna and the Penna described as "poems in concrete" were built more than a century ago.

Mineral Resources

Andhra Pradesh is a mineral rich state ranking second in the country. The state accounts for considerable reserves of important minerals, 42 in numbers.

Agriculture

It's the lifeline of state economy contributing over a third of the gross state domestic product and providing a livelihood for over 70 per cent of the population. However, landlessness is high, and statistics show that 10 per cent of the population holds 44 per cent of land.

Bio Resources

There are seven agro-climatic zones across the state with 19 major food and commercial crops grown in different parts of the state. There are more than 5,000 species of trees. About 40 per cent of the land is utilised for agriculture, and 23 per cent of the land is covered by forests in the state. The state has a strong base in horticulture, producing a variety of fruits and vegetables.

Women's Participation in Agriculture

In Andhra Pradesh women spend far more time in agricultural activities than men, however, they are paid much lower wages for the same work. Women are not given the status of farmers in their own right.

(B) UTTAR PRADESH

Location

Uttar Pradesh is truly the heartland of India situated in northern India and shares its border with Himachal Pradesh, Punjab, Delhi, Madhya Pradesh, Bihar and International border with Nepal. It lies between Latitude of 24° to 31° and Longitude of 77° to 54° easts.

Area

Uttar Pradesh has an area of 2.94 million sq. km. area-wise it is the 4th largest state.

Physiography

Uttar Pradesh can be divided into three distinct regions:

1. The Himalayan region in the north
2. The Gangetic plain in the center
3. The Vindhya Hills and plateau in the south

Climate

The climate of the State is tropical monsoon, but variants exist because of difference in altitude. The Himalayan region is cold. The average temperature varies in the plains from three to four degree centigrade in January to 43 to 45 degree centigrade in May and June. There are three distinct seasons, the cold season from October to February, summer from March to mid-June and the rainy season from March to September.

Soils

The Valley area has fertile and rich soil. There is an intensive cultivation on terraced hill slopes. The higher altitudes are suitable for subtropical and temperate fruit-culture.

Hills

The prominent peaks in the hill region include Banarpunch, Mount Kamety, Trishul, Dunagiri, Nandadevi, Badrinath and Kedarnath. The hill areas are sparsely populated. Due to the excessive nature of the terrain, soil is subject to heavy erosion.

Rivers

The major rivers are the Ganga, Yamuna, Gomti, Ghaghra, Rapti, Sharda and Ramganga.

Population

According to the 2001 census there are 166,052,859 persons in Uttar Pradesh of which 87,466,301 are males and 78,856,558 are females. The sex ratio (females per thousand males) is 898.

Characteristics of People

The central fact of the social order in Uttar Pradesh is the existence of the caste system among the Hindus who constitute the vast majority of the population. The broad hierarchy in the Hindu social system was the Brahmins, Kshatriyas, Vaisyas, Shudras and Achhuts (untouchables). Further division-based on occupation gave rise to casts like Nai (barber), Dhobi (Washerman), Lohar (blacksmith), Darzi (Tailor) and all of them formed a vital part of the village economy and life.

Structure of the Society

The village is the lynchpin of the state's economy. An assorted, shapeless, cluster of mud huts, roofs with thatch or khaprail (earthen tiles) with hardly any sanitation drainage or lighting arrangements and only narrow footpaths leading to the outside world constitute a typical Uttar Pradesh village.

Land is the status symbol in the village while the land owners generally are from the higher castes, it is their position as land owners which gives them status and power rather than their caste affiliation. Since independence, the concept of welfare state, zamindari abolition, the latest result of science and technology has benefitted the village.

A three-tier democracy is at work in the countryside. At the district level is the Zilla Parishad, at the block level, the Kshetra Samiti and at the village level, the Panchayat. To solve minor disputes there is the Nyaya Panchayat or the Village Court. All these are statutory bodies and form what is called the Panchayati Raj.

Election to the panchayats is by adult franchise and secret direct vote. Election to the Kshetra Samitis is by indirect vote, panchayat in a block constituting the Electoral College. The Zila Parishad has both ex-officio members and elected members. The ex-officio members include the members of the Parliament, Assembly and the Council of the District. A lot of government money in the shape of loans, assistance and advances for rural development is funneled through these institutional bodies into the villages.

The Nyaya Panchayat performs certain statutory functions in village disputes but it is the caste panchayats among the backward classes and Scheduled Caste which are more formidable. Most caste disputes are settled by them. They help to alleviate the difficulties of poor families to some extent, fixing limits to dowries, the number of persons to participate in marriage party and so on. They also regulate the customary dues involved in the system of Jajmani relationship.

Cultural Heritage

Hindu civilisation and culture reached its zenith in the territory of Uttar Pradesh. Some scholars are of the view that the Rigveda was composed in the Gangetic valley. It is generally accepted that a substantial portion of the vedic literature had its origin, here in its many hermitages, which were seats of learning. Some of the big names in Hindu sacred literature such as Yagnavalkya, Vashishta, Vishwamitra, Valmiki, Attriyea, Bhardwaj, Kapil and Vyas lived in these retreats of Uttar Pradesh and inspired millions through the ages.

Uttar Pradesh's greatest gifts to humanity are the two epics, Ramayana and Mahabharata. From the epic age, the territory of Uttar Pradesh is being watered by several fresh streams of culture, the two most significant being those generated by the teachings of Buddha and Mahavira, the 24th Jain Tirthankar. Manifestations of these are to be found in a mass of literature and numerous relics of art and architecture which form part of the precious cultural heritage of the country.

Schedule Castes

History has referred to Dalits as people without a history of their own. They have been marginalised as objects in a country rather than being treated as its subject; objects of philanthropic and social work rather than as subjects of a nation, who have equal rights as other citizens to all the benefits. Rather than that they have been pushed around and subjugated and exploited at every point in their life. Thus, their status needs to be lifted and all the atrocities meted out against them, put to a check. For this, we need certain strict measures to uplift them through sanctions by law, which give them a chance to avail benefits and facilities like reservation in employment and education and thus emancipate themselves further in the mainstream of the country.

Scheduled Tribes

The Scheduled Tribes account for a sizeable proportion of the population of India. They constitute an important segment of the Indian Social fabric. These communities belong to different ethno-lingual groups and profess different faiths. Living at disparate levels of socio-economic development, they are spread along the entire spectrum of social evolution in India ranging from the Paleolithic hunters and gatherers of forest produce to the industrial workers. Their spatial distribution is characterised by a striking tendency of clustering and concentration in pockets which have suffered from isolation historically.

Other Backward Classes

The question of reservation for backward castes (other backward classes) became prominent only after independence at national level by appointing Kaka Kalelkar Commission in 1953 and then B.P. Mandal Commission in 1978. Social distance between forward castes and backward castes (class) exist in Indian society in the form of Social inequality. By acceptance of Mandal Commission recommendations OBCs were granted 27 per cent quota in education and jobs.

Education

Number of recognised Educational Institutional Universities 17, Institutions deemed to be Universities-7, Degree Colleges - 1216.

Literacy Rate

2001 –

Persons	–	57 per cent
Male	–	70 per cent
Female	–	43 per cent

Number of Literates

2001 –

Persons	–	77,770,275
Males	–	50,256,119
Females	–	27,514,156

Transport and Communication

Road Transport: Uttar Pradesh has a well laid-out road network throughout the State totalling 78,482 km, out of which over 11,000 km. constitute National and State highways. The road network caters to a high level of passenger and freight movement.

Railways: The State is also extensively covered by the Indian Railways, which is easily one of the largest networks in the world. The headquarters of the North-Eastern Railway, an important constituent of Indian Railways is also located in the state Railways route length in Uttar Pradesh is 8901 km.

Airways: With airports located in the cities of Lucknow, Kanpur, Allahabad, Gorakhpur, Agra, Pant Nagar and Rae Barelli, the State is adequately covered by air services.

Inland water transport: Uttar Pradesh has a wide network of navigable river systems with high potential for Inland Water Transport.

Other Communication

Number of Post Offices	:	19,936

Language and Literature

In successive centuries after Buddha, Ayodhya, Prayag, Varanasi, Mathura and several other cities continued to play important role in the making of religious and cultural history in India. Several kings who ruled the region became immortal because of vedic rituals performed by them and patronage extended by them to learning.

Scholars like Ashwaghosh, Kalidas, Ban, Mayur, Diwakar, Vakpati, Bhavbuti Rajshe Khar, Laxmidhar, Mr Harsh and Krishna Misra adorned their province.

Medical Facilities

Number of Hospitals	:	735
Number of Dispensaries	:	1750

Life in Uttar Pradesh is short and uncertain. Female expects to live less than 55 years and the under five mortality rate is as high as 141 per thousand. Uttar Pradesh has the highest, less than five mortality rate, the second highest crude death rate and the third lowest life expectancy figure. Among all the major Indian States, Uttar Pradesh has the highest birth rate and the highest fertility rate.

Road

The State has an extensive network of roads and bridges. During last five years the expansion of the road system in Uttar Pradesh has been at par with the National Average.

Telecommunication

Free government land for upgradation of telecom infrastructure.

Air Transport

Three Aerodromes and 23 Air strips have been constructed all over the State. The Airport Authority of India has also been approached for the upgradation of Lucknow, Agra and Varanasi Airports, so that they could handle International Charters and Cargo.

Factors of Production

Land, Capital, Entrepreneurship, Manpower and Technology are the main factors of production. The State will facilitate the access of industry to these factors at competitive rates.

Tax System

Simplification and rationalisation of the tax system, State's commitment to low taxation and high compliance regime.

Entrepreneurship

The training of first generation Entrepreneurs must be given the highest priority by the State. The Institute of Entrepreneurship Development will be strengthened and streamlined so that it becomes an effective medium of entrepreneurship development in the State. Curriculum for these training programmes will be developed with the assistance of expert agencies. The State Financial Institutions will accord priority to trained applicants in the sanction of loans.

Human Resource Development and Technology

- Priority to training of youths whose land is acquired for Industrial purposes.
- Expertise of Technical Institutions to be thrown open for use by industry.
- System of Deemed Approvals System of Automatic Approvals for Industrial building maps.
- Synergy between Technical Institutions and Industry.

Thrust Area

Selected Industries to be developed as thrust sector:

- Agro-based and Food Processing Industry,
- Automobile Industry,
- Automobile Ancillaries,
- Electronics,
- Software,
- Engineering Goods,
- Agricultural Equipments Industry,
- All EOUS.

Small Industries

- Technology mission for small and village Industries.
- Equity participation by State Government in private marketing companies.
- District industries to help small industries in accessing information and latest technologies.

Finance Sector

No. of Societies : Credit - 11,471
Non-credit - 23,915

Tourism

Tourist Destinations:

River Ganga,
Agra,
Taj Mahal,
Akbar's Tomb,
Taj Mahal Museum,
Itlmad-Ud-Daulah Tomb,
Dayal Bagh Temple,
Agra Fort,
Fatehpur Sikri,
Jodha Bai's Palace,
Corbett National Park,
Mussoorie,
Keoladeo National Park,
Bharatpur,
Varanasi,
Kedareshwara Temple,
Vishwanath Temple,
(Golden Temple),
Alamgir Mosque,

District Profile

B-I. Bareilly

According to 2001Census, Bareilly had a total population of 3,618,589 out of which 1,934,119 are males while 1,684,470 are females.

Rural population was 2,427,139 out of which 1,303,590 were males while 1,123,549 were females.

Urban population was 1,191,450 out of which 6,30,529 were males while 5,60,921 were females.

Hindus constitute 64.81 per cent of the total population;

Muslims constitute 33.89 per cent of the total population;

Christians constitute 0.26 per cent of the total population;

Sikhs constitute 0.80 per cent of the total population;

Buddhists constitute 0.21 per cent of the total population;

Jains constitute 0.02 per cent of the total population;

Other religions constitute 0.00 per cent of the total population;

Religions not stated constitute 0.02 per cent of the total population;

Scheduled Castes constitutes 12.65 per cent of the total population.. Rural 15.19 per cent, Urban 7.48 per cent of SC population. According to 2001 Census, Bareilly had a total SC population of 457,771 out of which 246,091 were males while 211,680 were female.

Schedules tribes constitute 0.01 per cent of the total population 0.00 per cent of the rural areas and 0.03 per cent of the urban area population. Bareilly had a total population of 375 (ST) out of which 205 were males and 170 were females.

Parliamentary and Assembly Constituencies of State

Bareilly 51, Bareilly Cantonment 52, Bareilly City 53
Nawabganj 54, Bhojpure and 55, Kawar

Name of Districts, Tehsils and Towns (2001)

District	:	Bareilly
Sub-District	:	Baheri
Sub-District	:	Meerganj
Sub-District	:	Aonla
Sub-District	:	Bareilly
Sub-District	:	Nawabganj
Sub-District	:	Faridpur
Town	:	Bareilly

List of Administrative Districts (2001)

State/District	*Capital/ District Headquarters*	*Area in sq. km.*	*Population*
Bareilly	Bareilly	4,120	35,98,701

Education

Mahatma Jyotiba Phule Rohilkhand University (Estd. 1975); Bareilly; Jurisdiction: The Jurisdiction of the University extends to the districts of Bijnor, Moradabad, Rampur, Bareilly, Shahjahanpur, Buden and Pilibhit. There are 63 affiliated colleges.

Industry

Multi-national, Private and Public Companies, Indian Farmers Fertilizers Ammonia, Urea Allahabad, Bareilly.

Name of Dam-Dhara; Year of completion: 1961: River- Dhara: Nearest City- Bareilly.

Name of Dam Baigul; Year of Completion 1968: River- Baigul; Nearest City Bareilly.

Hotels

Bareilly, Taj Residency.

Five Star Access: 18-km., Amausi Airport 5 km, from Railway Station, 4 km. From City Centre, Rooms: 110.

Big Dailies

Title: Dainik Jagran - Hindi - Bareilly - 82329

Big Periodicals

Title - Sheetal Group Samvaad Kesri - Hindi - Weekly - Bareilly - 76013

Medium Dailies

Title - Amar Ujala - Hindi - Bareilly - 56269

Title - Lucknow Mail - Hindi - Bareilly - 27814

Title - Sheetal Group Samvaad Kesri

Hindi - Bareilly - 34477

Small Dailies

Title - Aaj - Hindi - Bareilly - 22,519

Title - Tarjumaan - E- Bareilly - Urdu - Bareilly - 6,154

Small Periodicals - Quami Hamdard - Urdu - Weekly - Bareilly - 58825

Tarjuman-E-Bareilly - Urdu - Weekly - Bareilly - 3,125

Tarj Karan - Urdu - Weekly - Bareilly - 7,400

Parwaz-E-Watan - Urdu - Weekly - Bareilly - 3,100

Adal-ki-Awaj - Urdu - Weekly - Bareilly - 3,950

Hubbe Watan - Urdu - Weekly - Bareilly - 2,617

Gorakhpur

According to 2001 census Gorakhpur had a total population of 3,769,456, out of which 1,923,197 were males and 1,846,259 were females.

Rural population was 3,030,865 while urban population was 738,591.

Hindus constitute 90.39 per cent of the total population;

Muslims constitute 9.15 per cent of the total population;

Christians constitute 0.17 per cent of the total population;

Sikhs constitute 0.09 per cent of the total population;

Buddhists constitute 0.15 per cent of the total population;

Jains constitute 0.01 per cent of the total population;

Other Religions constitute 0.00 per cent of the total population.

Religions not stated constitute 0.04 per cent of the total population.

Scheduled Castes constitute 22.05 per cent of the total population, Rural (SCs) 24.37 per cent, Urban (SCs) 12.52 per cent, Scheduled Tribes constitutes 0.02 per cent of the total population, Rural 0.02 per cent, Urban 0.04 per cent.

B-II. Gorakhpur

The following are the Sub-districts in Gorakhpur:

Sub-District	:	Campierganj
Sub-District	:	Sahjanwa
Sub-District	:	Gorakhpur
Sub-District	:	Chauri Chaura
Sub-District	:	Bansgaon
Sub-District	:	Khajni
Sub-District	:	Gola

List of Administrative Districts (2001)

State/District	*Capital/ District Headquarters*	*Area in sq. km.*
Gorakhpur	Gorakhpur	3,321

Education

Deendayal Upadhyaya Gorakhpur University, (Estd. 1957) Gorakhpur; Jurisdiction of the University extends to the districts of Gorakhpur, Deoria, Basti, Siddhartha Nagar, Maharajganj, Sant Kabir Nagar and Kushi Nagar. The university has four professional colleges and 82 affiliated colleges.

Industry

Development of Geographical Nodes/Industrial Corridor:

1. Gorakhpur - Basti - Deoria (Industrial corridor)

Hotels (Tourism)

Carlton Hotel Private Limited; 3 Star accesses 13 km from Airport, and 4 km from Railway Station, 1 km from Downtown Area-Rooms: 30.

District Profile

A-I. Rangareddi District

Population

According to 2001 census, Rangareddi had a total population of 3,575,064, out of which 1,839,227 were males and 1,735,837 were females.

Rural population was 1,637,227 while urban population was 1,937,837.

Religion-wise Distribution

Hindus constitute 85.62 per cent of the total population;

Muslims constitute 11.41 per cent of the total population;

Christians constitute 2.51 per cent of the total population;

Sikhs constitute 0.18 per cent of the total population;

Buddhists constitute 0.05 per cent of the total population;

Jains constitute 0.05 per cent of the total population;

Other religions constitute 0.03 per cent of the total population;

Religions not stated constitute 0.15 per cent of the total population;

SC population ratio w.r.t. population (2001);

Scheduled Castes constitute 14.55 per cent of the total population - 20.59 per cent - Urban, 9.44 per cent - Rural.

ST Population Ratio w.r.t. population (2001);

STs constitute 4.09 per cent of the total population, 7.32 per cent - Urban, 1.36 per cent - Rural.

District - Rangareddi

Sub-Districts:

Marapalle, Mominpet, Nawabget, Shankerpalle, Serilingampally, Balanagar, Qutubullapur, Medchal, Shamirpet, Malkajgiri, Keesara, Ghat Kesar, Uppal, Hayath Nagar, Saroor Nagar, Rajendra Nagar, Moinabad, Cherella, Vicarabad, Dharur, Bantwaran, Peddemul, Tandur, Basheerabad, Yelal, Doma, Gandedd, Kulkacharla, Pargi, Pudur, Shabad, Shamsabad, Maheswaram, Kandukur, Ibrahim Patnam, Manchal, Yacharam.

Town

Serilingampally, Ram Chandra Puram, (BHEL township), Kukat Pally, Qutubullapur, Alwal, Alwar, Malkajgiri, Kapra, Uppal Kalan,

Gaddiannaram, Lal Bahadur Nagar, Lal Bahadur Nagar Part, Meerpet, Rajendra Nagar, Rajendra Nagar Part.

List of Administrative Districts (2001)

State/District	*Capital/ District Headquarters*	*Area in sq. km.*	*Population*
Rangareddi	Rangareddi	7.5	35,87,891

District-wise distribution of Commercial Banks and average population per Bank

District	*Rural*	*Semi-Urban*	*Urban*	*Metropolitan/ Part Town*	*Total*	*Average Population per Bank Office (in 6000)*
Rangareddi	80	52	47	—	179	20

B-II. Chittoor Population

According to 2001 census Chittoor had a total population of 3,745,875, out of which 1,889,690 were males while 1,856,185 were females.

Rural population was 2,934,845 while urban population was 811,030.

Religion-wise Distribution

Hindus constitute 89.91 per cent of the total population;

Muslims constitute 09.15 per cent of the total population;

Christians constitute 0.76 per cent of the total population;

Sikhs constitute 0.04 per cent of the total population;

Buddhists constitute 0.01 per cent of the total population;

Jains constitute 0.03 per cent of the total population;

Other Religions constitute 0.00 per cent of the total population;

Religions not stated constitute 0.11 per cent of the total population;

Scheduled Castes constituted 18.75 per cent of the total population;

Rural SCs constituted 21.11 per cent of population, Urban SCs - 10.19 per cent of population.

Scheduled Tribes constituted 3.42 per cent of the total population, Rural STs constituted 3.81 per cent of the population, Urban STs constituted 2.00 per cent of the population.

Parliamentary Constituencies and Assembly Constituencies of the State

Chittoor - 139, Vepanjer (SC) 140 - Chittoor, 141- Palmaner (SC), 142 - Kuppam, 143 - Punganur, 147 - Pileru and 148 - Chandraganj.

Name of State, Districts, Tehsils and Towns

District: Chittoor

Sub-Districts

Mulakalacheruvu, Thamballapalle Peddamandyam, Gurram Konda, Kala Kada, Kambhanvanipalle, Rompicherla, Yerra Varipalem, Tirupati (Rural), Renigunta, Yerpedu, Srikalahasti, Thottambedu, Budhinaidu Kandriga, Varadaiahpalem, K.V.B. Puram, Tirupati (Urban), Chandragiri.

Sub-Districts

Chinnagottigallu, Pilar, Kalikuri, Vayalpad, Kurabalak, Pedda thippa Samudram, B. Kothakota, Madanapalle, Nimmanapalle, Sodam, Pulicheria, Pakala, Veduru, Kupram, Ram Chandra Puram, Vadama lapeta, Narayanavanam, Pichatum, Satyaredu, Nagalapuram, Nindra, Vijayapuram, Nagari, Puttur, Karvefi Nagar, Penumuru, Puthalapattu, Irala, Somala, Chowdepalle, Rama Sundaram, Purganur, Peddapanjani, Gangavaram, Thavananpalie, Sriranporajapuram, Gangadhara Nellero, Chittoor, Palamaner, Baireddipalle, Venkatagiri Kotam, Santhipuram, Gudupalle, Kuppam, Ramakuppam, Bargarupalem, Yadamam, Gudipale, Palasamudram.

Town: Tirchanur, Tirupati, Akkarampalle, Madanapalle.

State/District	*Capital/ District Headquarters*	*Area in sq. km.*
Chittoor	Gorakhpur	15.2

District-wise Distribution of Commercial Banks and Average Population per Bank in Andhra Pradesh.

District	*Rural*	*Semi-Urban*	*Urban*	*Metropolitan/ Port Town*	*Total*	*Average Population per Bank Office (in 6000)*
Chittoor	127	59	64	—	250	15

Dams

Name of the Dam: Mallemadugu; Year of completion - 1959, River - Mallemadugu, nearest city - Chittoor.

Name of the Dam Kalyan; Year of completion 1978; River Kalyana: nearest city Chittoor.

Name of the Dam Peddere; Reservoir, River Pedduru, nearest city—Chittoor.

These are in brief the profile of the area of the study we have undertaken.

3

The District Planning Committees: The Composition and Working

For the last several decades efforts have been on to decentralise planning for achieving goals of development in the rural sector. We have discussed the importance of decentralised planning for rural development and the effort that has gone into this in the preceding pages. We now propose to specifically focus on the composition and working of the District Planning Committees through which the decentralised planning has supposedly been made operative. It may be noted here that the exercise of planning from below in the form of Block Level Planning and the District Planning was initiated quite early in our planning process. However, the present exercise through the District Planning Committees is supposed to be different in many respects which we would try to analyse in the present chapter.

The present composition of the District Planning Committee owes its origin to the Article 243-ZD of the Constitution of India. The aforesaid Article provides that there shall be constituted in every State at the district level a District Planning Committee to consolidate the plan prepared by the Panchayats and the Municipalities in the district and to prepare a draft development plan for the district as a whole. The Constitution further provides that the Legislature of a State may, by law, make provisions with respect to.

(a) The composition of the District Planning Committees;

(b) The manner in which the seats in such committees shall be filled:

Provided that not less than four-fifths of the total number of members of such Committees shall be elected by, and from amongst, the elected members of the Panchayats at district level and of the Municipalities in the district in proportion to the ratio between the population of the rural areas and of the urban areas in the district.

(c) The function relating to district planning which may assigned to such Committees.

(d) The manner in which the Chairperson of such Committees shall be chosen.

The Constitution further indicates that every District Planning Committee shall, in preparing the draft development plan:

(i) It's matters of common interest between the Panchayat and the Municipalities including spatial planning, sharing of water and other physical and natural resources, the integrated development of infrastructure and environmental conservation.

(ii) The extent and type of available resources whether financial or otherwise.

(iii) Consult such institutions and organisations as the Governor may by order, specify.

After these Constitutional Amendments were made effective, it was the responsibility of the State governments to make suitable amendments in their laws dealing with the Panchayats and the Municipalities. Several State governments took steps to suitably amend the laws governing these bodies and issued Government Orders to constitute District Planning Committees as per the norms provided by the Amendment Act of 1994.

So far as the composition of the District Planning Committees is concerned, they are generally composed of elected members of the local bodies within the district, both rural and urban, as well as some nominated members. The number of members varies with the population size of the districts. The ratio of members from Panchayats and urban local bodies is based on the ratio in which the population of the district is divided between rural and urban areas.

- It may be noted here that an examination of the composition of the District Planning Committees is vital from different perspective. There could be several factors which affect the composition of the District Planning Committee in the State, and we would focus on those factors while examining the composition of the District Planning Committees across the States.

It is a matter of concern that even after the lapse of almost twenty years since the Amendments were made, the decentralised planning is yet to become really effective in the country. While most of the States carried out the Amendments of their respective State Acts governing these institutions in conformation of the 73rd and 74th Amendments, the implementation of provisions was not uniform in all cases. Setting up elected local bodies in local self-governance institutions was carried out and State Finance Commissions were also formed to provide for financial devolution to these local bodies. However, formation of District Planning Committees was one of the neglected aspects. The issue of decentralised planning was discussed at the Second Round Table Meeting of the State Ministers of Panchayat, Panchayati Raj held in Mupore in 2004. The recommendations that emerged from the meeting included the resolution for constituting District Planning Committees in all the States by the end of 2004-05. The States were also required to outline their functions and procedures, and to identify agencies which will assist in the district planning process. The States were recommended to provide resources in the form of untied funds to Panchayats and Municipalities to strengthen their finances. The Planning Commission was also requested to ensure that the Eleventh Plan is based on consolidation of District Plans prepared through District Planning Committees.

The Expert Group for Planning at Grassroots level, chaired by V. Ramchandran was set up in 2005 and set forth an action plan in order to strengthen participatory planning in the Eleventh Plan process. It noted with concern the fact that several States had not set up District Planning Committees even after the resolution taken in the Second Round Table. The Group laid out the modalities of preparing perspective five-year and annual plans at the district level and gave further suggestions for strengthening the District Planning Committees. The Report contemplated that the District Planning Committees should be a permanent institution provided with a secretariat to support its functioning. The District Planning

Committees should be the nodal agency for district level planning, and planning tasks including those relating to Central Plan schemes, need to be routed through the District Planning Committees. The District Planning Committee can take the assistance of technical and academic institutions and experts to perform its functions effectively. The group laid out detailed guidelines for the district level planning process and the role of the District Planning Committees therein.

It may be noted here that the Planning Commission took action on these proposals and communicated to the States that the approval of the Annual Plan proposals for 2006-07 will be contingent upon the constitution of District Planning Committees in all the districts. The Annual Plan Proposal must give details of the total fund availability from various sources down to the Panchayat level. They must indicate the detailed deployment of funds received from various sources among the district and must also explain the criteria followed for allocating the resources. The preparation of annual planning exercise under the Eleventh Plan is thus expected to activate the process of district planning across all the States.

Another significant measure to push for the activation of District Planning Committees is the linking of access to the Backward Region Grants Funds (BRGF) scheme. It is a semi-tried fund available to 250 selected backward districts with the purpose of cataloging development by providing infrastructure, promoting good governance and agrarian reforms and capacity building for participatory district planning. In order to avail BRGF funds, the States are required to establish District Planning Committee as per Article 243ZD, which will consolidate plans prepared by PRIs and ULBs in the district. These plans will put together resources from various existing schemes and channelise them to Panchayats on the basis of the District Plan. The BRGF funds will be used by the Panchayats for gap filling and to converging and add value to other programmes which provide much larger resources to the same district. The formula for the reimbursement of BRGF fund within the district will also be derived at the local level.

Taking into account the rendered effort towards achieving effective planning at the grassroots level through the District Planning Committees, it is worth noting the status of the District Planning Committees which have been so far formed across the country. In this respect PRIA presents a detailed analysis of the status of the DPCs across different States in India. Twelve States in

Himachal Pradesh, Haryana, Rajasthan, Uttar Pradesh, Uttarakhand, Bihar, Jharkhand, Chhattisgarh, Madhya Pradesh, Gujarat, Andhra Pradesh, and Kerala are the states covered for detailed primary investigation into the states of DPCs, since the PRIA has a direct or indirect presence in these States. The Report highlights the gap between what appears on paper and what the actual situation is on the ground for these States.

Status of District Planning Committees across States

As reported earlier the District Planning Committees were to be constituted as per Article 243ZD of the Constitution in all the States except Jammu and Kashmir, Meghalaya, Mizoram, Nagaland and the NCT of Delhi. All States must accordingly enact legislations for constitution of DPCs and issue notification bringing them into effect.

The expert Group Report of 2006 also carried out a status check on the constitution of DPC, across the States. It may, however, be noted that things have not changed significantly since then. Their findings for 19 major States, updated till recently, are listed in the Table 3.1 below:

Table 3.1. Status of DPC Formation Across States

Sl. No.	*States / UTs*	*Status of Constitution of DPCs in May 2006*	*Status in November 2007*
1.	Andhra Pradesh	Not yet constituted	Elections held in April 2007, but DPCs not functional
2.	Assam	Not yet constituted	Constituted in all non-sixth schedule districts
3.	Bihar	Constituted with President ZP as Chairperson	No change
4.	Chhattisgarh	Constituted with Minister as Chairperson of DPC	All members nominated by State Government
5.	Gujarat	Not yet constituted	Constituted
6.	Haryana	Constituted in all districts	No change
7.	Himachal Pradesh	Constituted with Minister as Chairperson of DPC	No change
8.	Jharkhand	Local body elections yet to be held	No change
9.	Karnataka	Constituted with President ZP as Chairperson	No change

10.	Kerala	Constituted with Chairman District Panchayat as Chairperson	No change
11.	Madhya Pradesh	Constituted with district in-charge Minister as Chairperson of DPC	No change
12.	Maharashtra	Not yet constituted	Constituted with district in-charge Minister as Chairperson of DPC
13.	Orissa	Constituted in 26 districts with Minster as Chairperson	Constituted in all 30 districts with Minister as Chairperson
14.	Punjab	Not yet constituted	Constituted with Ministers as Chairperson/Vice Chairperson
15.	Rajasthan	Constituted with Chairman District Panchayat as Chairperson	No change
16.	Tamil Nadu	Constituted with Chairman District Panchayat as Chairperson	No change
17.	Uttar Pradesh	Not notified though legal provision exists	No change
18.	Uttarakhand	Not notified though legal provision exists	No change
19.	West Bengal	Constituted with Chairman District Panchayat as Chairperson	No change

Source: Report of Expert Group on Grassroots Planning and PRIA

It may be noted here that most of the major States in the country have constituted the District Planning Committees as per the information available. State's legislation to constitute DPCs has been enacted in all the States considered here. Interestingly the State of Uttar Pradesh, Uttarakhand and Jharkhand were quite late in constituting the DPCs despite repeated instructions from the Government of India.

In Uttar Pradesh, the constitution of District Planning Committee by the current government got delayed on account of a minor change desired by it in the composition of the DPC. Earlier, the Minister-in-Charge of the district was the Chairman of the DPC and there were two Deputy Chairperson – The Zila Panchayat President and the Chief Executive Officer of the Municipality within the district. The current Government wanted to remove the urban representation as the post of the Deputy Chairperson of the DPC. The existing structure for district level planning in the State is the District Planning and Monitoring Committee or the DPMC. The DPMC is chaired by the Minister-in-Charge and the President of the Zila Panchayat also finds a representation in it. The meetings of DPMC are actually chaired by the District Magistrate (DM) and the Minister-in-Charge is rarely present. It is a purely administrative structure meant for disbursing Plan, fund and deciding scheme specific allocations. Since the prevailing DPMC system is concurrent politically as well, there seems to be no real pressure on the State government to expedite the constitution of DPCs. This could be major factor for the delay on the part of the State government to constitute the DPCs in the State.

Composition of District Planning Committees

The District Planning Committees are generally comprised elected members of the local bodies within the district, both rural and urban, as well as some nominated members. The number of members varies with the population size of the district. The ratio of members from Panchayats and Urban Local Bodies is based on the ratio in which the population of the district is divided between rural and urban areas.

An analysis of the Corporation of the District Planning Committee is important from two perspectives:

- It reflects the degree of inclusion of marginalised sections in the district planning process.
- It reflects the degree to which the District Planning Committee is actually a body independent of State control and interference.

We now take the discussion further keeping in view of these two broad perspectives.

Elections to District Planning Committees

The information collected from most of the States show that elections have been held for the Constitution of District Planning Committees. However, whether or not they were actually held is another question altogether. Election has mostly been supervised by district administration or State Government such elections are highly doubtful. In Gujarat, for example, elections were supposed to be held but some of the members are not aware of their membership in the District Planning Committees. Similar situation is reported in Haryana. In Chhattisgarh, in spite of the existing legislation, elections were not held at all. Yet, the DPCs were constituted. The following Table 3.2 shows the agencies responsible for supervising the elections to the DPCs.

Table 3.2. Agencies Responsible for Supervising DPC Elections

Supervising Agency/Officer	*States*
District Collector	Madhya Pradesh, Andhra Pradesh
State Government	Gujarat, Karnataka
State Election Commission	Kerala, Bihar
Deputy Commissioner	Haryana, Himachal Pradesh

Source: Various State Acts/Notification/PRIA survey.

It could well be seen from the table above that there is no uniformity so far as the agencies supervising the elections to the District Planning Committees. In this context, it is argued that the State Election Commission would be the most desirable agencies for conducting DPC election, as they are expected to be more impartial than other agencies and official of the State government. It may be pointed out here that in Kerala in fact, DPC elections are synchronised with local government elections. This alternative is worth giving a trial by other states which may avoid unnecessary delay and bickering caused by such delays.

Composition of Elected and Nominated Members

Under the provisions of Article 243ZD the District Planning Committees are to have at least four-fifth-elected members. The Members ought to elected by, and from amongst, the elected member of the Panchayat at the district level and of the municipalities in the district in proportion to the ratio between the population of the rural area and of the urban areas in the district. Traversal pattern, however, varies across states.

Nominated members usually represent the State and Central Government agencies (including five departments). A larger proportion of nominated members could imply greater influences and control in the functioning of the DPC by the State and Central administration. This is in effect erodes the participative nature of the Committees, reducing it to just another arm of the State administration. It may therefore, be impressed here that the proportion of nominated members should not increase beyond the figure, Constitution stipulated the limit.

Chairperson of District Planning Committees

The Chairperson of the District Planning Committees and the manner, in which he/she is appointed, is also an indicator of the degree to which the DPC is actually an independent body. In this respect, three different patterns are observed among the States:

- In some states the Chairperson/President/CEO or the Zila Parishad or District Panchayat in the Chairperson of the DPC as well, for example Kerala, Andhra Pradesh, Rajasthan, Tamil Nadu and West Bengal.
- In some states the Minister-in-Charge of the district or any other State Minister is the Chairperson, for example in Orissa, Gujarat, Madhya Pradesh, Chhattisgarh, and Maharashtra. In Himachal Pradesh, Cabinet Minister of the State Government have been nominated as member and Chairperson of the DPCs.
- In Haryana the Deputy Commissioner (DC) of the district is the Chairperson of the DPC.

It is being realised that having the Minister-in-Charge or any Minister from the State Cabinet as the Chairperson of the DPC ensures that the DPC work only as an arm of the State Government with little capacity for independent functioning Members in such Committees are liable to be dominated by the Minister. The mere presence of the Minister changes the functioning environment. No decision can be taken in such a Committee which is against the policy of the State government.

The Functions and the Working of District Planning Committee

It is worth recalling here that the District Planning Committee is envisaged to play a model role in the district planning process, by consolidating rural and urban plans prepared by the villages and towns in the district and then preparing a draft development plan for the district on the basis of the plans also received from within the district. The District Planning Committee is, thus, crucial to the function of 'planning for economic and social justice', which is now a mandated local function, in that it provides the vital limits between rural and urban plans as well as sectoral plans. In this respect it is important that the DPCs have an understanding of the planning process and the assistance of qualified planner and technical experts. As per Article 243ZD, the DPCs should also pay special regard to issue of common interest between Panchayats and Municipalities, such as spatial planning, sharing of physical and natural resources, infrastructure development and environmental conservation. Since the States have modelled their own legislative provisions for DPCs on Article 243ZD, the role and function of DPCs in the State Acts are, by and large, similar.

Consolidation of Rural and Urban Plans

As noted earlier, consolidation of rural and urban plans, is one of the by tasks of the District Planning Committee and is also of great importance in the light of growing problem related to urban experience into rural areas. The sequence to be followed in consolidation of rural and urban plans can be summarised as following (PRIA, 2007):

- Gram Panchayats prepare participatory Plan and sent to Intermediate Panchayats; Intermediate Panchayat compiles information sent by the Gram Panchayat in the Blocks and along with its own information, prepares a Block Plan and sends it to Zila Panchayat.
- Zila Panchayat compiles information from Block Panchayats and along with its own information, sends it to the DPC.
- Urban Local Bodies transmit plan to DPCs.
- DPC compiles information from Zila Panchayat and ULBs to form Draft Development Plan (DDP).

During the course of the study information about consolidation of District plans was collected from various states. This shows that while the sequence of steps to be followed in consolidating rural and urban plans is similar, though the ground reality is entirely different. In Haryana, Andhra Pradesh and Chhattisgarh the DPCs were simply not functioning, therefore, we could not make any observation towards that. In Bihar, Gujarat and Himachal Pradesh allegedly no meetings have been effectively held since the constitution of DPCs, except the formal first meeting for oath taking. This only goes to suggest that though the DPCs were formally constituted they hardly remains effective in the real sense of the term.

For Madhya Pradesh too the situation is not very encouraging as no previous information on DPC meetings was available. However, the guidelines for decentralised planning process under the Eleventh

Plan period are available. The role of the DPC in the district planning process has been well defined. It says that the DPC will finalise sectoral plan allocation for rural and urban areas with the live department. The DPC should also assess available resources in the district with the help of an expert group which can include subject experts. This integrated district annual plan will then be submitted by the DPC to the State Planning Board. As per field information, this process does take place in the districts. However, the plan themselves are weak and lack any integrated approach. Planning has become more of a procedural formality than a meaningful planning.

The plan in Rajasthan are prepared sector-wise and area-wise by the DPCs as per the ceiling on budgeted amount fixed by the State Government. Proposals are invited from the heads of various departments and the funds are then disbursed accordingly. There are 17 sections which have been identified for preparation of district plan. It has been noted that the planning exercise for the year 2006-07 was carried out at the district level, but it was essentially an officer-based exercise.

In Karnataka, it is the sole responsibility of the District Planning Committee to prepare the district plan. The development plan has to be based on the perspective plan prepared by it. A separate urban unit has to be formed for preparation of urban plan. DPCs can seek the support of the experts and technical agencies for plan preparation. The DPC also needs to periodically evaluate progress of the plans and projects in the district and undertake studies on development indications. It is alleged that DPCs are not meeting as frequently as stipulated (PRIA, 2007).

The approach of Kerala is reportedly different from the states discussed earlier. Kerala's approach to initiating the process of grassroots planning was in the form of a year long People's Campaign for Planning, launched by the Kerala Planning Board. The Campaign mode helped build mass awareness and participation in the decentralised planning process when it was initiated for the first time in 1996. As per the current planning procedure in Kerala, at the intermediate level there is Technical Advisory Committee (TAC) to vet and verify the plans prepared by the Gram Panchayats and recommended to the DPC and the TAC then vets and verifies the plans. Integration is made at the instance of TAC and the Plan Preparation Support Group (PPSG). The DPC then consolidates this plans received from local bodies within the district and submit the same to the State Government.

From the discussion presented in the earlier pages, it can be seen that although the functions of DPCs have been already defined by the Constitution and have been adopted as such by most of the states, the functions are not being performed largely because of the DPCs not being functional themselves. The case of Kerala is an exception where the DPCs are active and functional institutions.

Technical Support to District Planning Committee

It is provided that the District Planning Committee can take the support of institutions as well as technical experts in the process of consolidating plan and preparing the draft development plan. Technical experts can also be nominated as member of the DPC. For example, in Haryana, the district Town Planner is a nominated member in 25-member Committee. Similarly, Chhattisgarh also provide for the membership of Economic and Statistical Officer of the district as a nominated member. In Kerala, the DPC is assisted in sensitising plans and profits by the Technical Advisory Committees (TACs). The TACs have sectoral sub-committee to study the respective chapters of the district plan. The DPC also consult with their working groups of technical experts as and when necessary.

If we look at some other states we find a different pattern. In Rajasthan, different means have been adopted by the DPCs for technical support. The plan consolidates work is being carried out by the Chief Planning Officer of the district. The DPC can also an expert as consultants. Heads of all line departments are often invited in DPC meetings. In Karnataka, DPCs can constitute expert committees and can also hire technical experts if they feel the need.

The recent measures taken by the Planning Commission and the Ministry of Panchayati Raj to activate the process of planning from below in a participative manner are indeed laudable. There is more so given the fact that even after about two decades since the enactment of the 73rd and 74th Amendment Acts, decentralised governance is yet to be realised. As per the Planning Commission: institutions issued to States on November 2006, regarding decentralised planning plans must be routed through DPCs, hence they are central to the district level planning process for the Eleventh Plan.

The inferences arrived at on the basis of our analysis are as follows (Planning Commission, 2001):

- The DPC is a vital link in the process of bottom-up planning. However, in spite of the various efforts taken over the years, DPCs are not functional in most of the states. In a few states, they are not even constituted, while in most states they are constituted but not in constitutionally desired ways (Minister as Chairperson or all members nominated by State Government). The scenario in ten of the states, on the basis of status and functioning of the DPCs, has been presented in this report in detail.
- States have generally followed Article 243ZD in fixing ratio of elected to nominated members, as well as in defining the functions and responsibilities of DPC.
- Chhattisgarh is a unique exception to the above case as all the members of DPC in the state are nominated by the state government — this is in violation of the state's own legal provision for DPCs.
- The system of having State Minister as Chairpersons of DPCs severely hampers the participative nature of the planning process in the DPC. This is corroborated by our study in Chhattisgarh where DPC members reported that decisions were unilaterally taken by the Minister-in-Charge of the district (who is the Chairperson) without heeding suggestions from other members. Hence, the decisions often did not reflect the popular opinion. This is a problem common to all states where ministers are chairpersons of DPC, such as Gujarat, Madhya Pradesh, Orissa, Maharashtra and Himachal Pradesh.
- Among the states considered in the study, DPCs are functioning effectively only in Kerala, and to some extent in Karnataka and Rajasthan, Kerala has in fact emerged as one of the foremost states where decentralised planning is in place and the DPCs are functioning satisfactorily. The decentralised planning process is, however, not devoid of state influence. Local bodies cannot initiate planning process till the State Government issues guidelines for plan preparation. These guidelines often contain sectoral priorities and key issues to be addressed along with methodological instructions. These are binding on all local bodies and hence may actually hinder the independent nature of people's planning.

- In Rajasthan, the role of DPCs appears focussed towards disbursement of united funds and implementation of plan schemes. It seems DPCs in Rajasthan are more like 'District Disbursement and Implementation Committees' rather than 'Planning' committees.
- DPCs have not been able to effectively enable rural-urban linkages. Coordinated planning is not taking place, and any joint project planning has not necessarily resulted in integrated project implementation. Several reasons account for this.

Rural and urban local bodies are not working together on a common platform during the planning process to identify common projects/resource requirements. The plans made in isolation cannot be implemented in an integrated manner. Urban local bodies have traditionally been oriented towards the State Directorate/ Departments of Urban Development — hence plans are submitted at the State level apex body for ULBs rather than DPCs — the vertical line of accountability still persists in spite of the revised planning process. This problem has been observed in district planning in Karnataka (Priya, 2007).

- Block level integration of rural and urban plans is not carried out the DPC guidelines recommend direct transmission of ULB plans to DPC. This may be a hindrance to effective integration of plans at the block level, which may be important especially in the case of small towns. These small towns have significant linkages with surrounding rural areas since they serve the purpose of market centers of the rural hinterland.
- Inter-sector coordination was also felt to be a problem since it was resisted on account of being against the status quo — old procedures are being followed for the sake of convenience as well. For example, the planning process of schemes like NREGA, SSA, NRHM and JNNURUM, wherever undertaken, is often independent of annual planning at Panchayat or Municipal levels.

Several concrete steps need to be taken to further strengthen and decentralise the institution of DPCs. In order to give them a truly representative and participatory shape it is extremely necessary that practices such as appointing State Ministers as Chairpersons, or nominating all members of DPC, be put an end to. The Government might consider introducing some disincentives for states adhering to such practices. Certain constructive measures that need to be taken in order to strengthen DPCs include the following (Kanan, 2000):

- The DPCs need to be given adequate financial support as well as staff strength in order to enable them to perform their tasks effectively. Converting DPCs into permanent institutions with offices and secretarial will perhaps address this issue to a large extent.
- Capacity building needs that emerge are pressing — the need for members to understand the true role of the DPC and what it seeks to achieve; the need for members as well as experts to understand the nuances of integrated planning for social and economic development and the difference between perspective plans.

The District Planning Committee, therefore, occupies an important place in the overall scheme of things so far as the decentralised planning is concerned. The analysis presented in the earlier pages briefly tries to bring into focus the theoretical as well as the practical status of the decentralised planning and the District Planning Committee in the country which does not point a very positive picture.

4

The Role of District Planning Committees in Decentralised Planning

The basic premise of decentralised planning and its evolution through different phases of India's planning process have briefly been discussed in the previous pages. We have also elaborated on the composition and working of the District Planning Committees in various states across the country. It is now proposed to discuss and briefly analyse the issues connected with decentralised planning vis-à-vis District Planning Committees with reference to the selected areas of our study. The observations here are based on the primary data collected through two questionnaires (copy enclosed as Annexure-I) administered on the officials and non-officials respectively connected with decentralised planning and the District Planning Committees apart from the observation notes prepared by the study team.

It may be pointed out that the data base regarding two selected states, viz., Andhra Pradesh and Uttar Pradesh constitutes both the primary as well as secondary. Owing to disturbances due to prolonged Telangana agitation, collection of data from the primary sources got hampered. Our observations for the State therefore, are based generally on the secondary sources which we could collect from various sources.

The Planning Process: The Non-official Response

In the preparation of plan the process occupies an important place as it determines the quality of the plan. With this in view the respondents were asked as to how far they are satisfied with the planning process in their State and the district. The responses received are given in the Table 1. These responses belong to the non-official connected with the decentralised planning process at different levels. The responses received from the official will be taken up after completing the discussion and the analysis of the responses of the non-official.

Table 1. Satisfaction Regarding the Planning Process

Extent	*Bareilly*		*Gorakhpur*	*U.P.*
	State	*District*	*State*	*District*
To a large extent	25	37.50	23.08	30.77
To some extent	62.50	37.50	46.15	57.85
Not at all	12.50	25.00	30.77	65.38
Total	**100.00**	**100.00**	**100.00**	**100.00**

It could be seen from the figure given in the table above that there are considerable variations so for as the question of satisfaction from the planning process is concerned. In Bareilly district, the majority of the respondents (62.5 per cent), reported that they are only 'to some extent' satisfied with the planning process at the State level while percentage of satisfaction is much lower (37.50 per cent) at the district level. The satisfaction category of 'not at all' at the state level is not high (12.50 per cent) but at the district level one-fourth of the respondents are reported in this category. It clearly indicates that the opinion of the respondents about the planning process at the district level deserves attention. In Gorakhpur districts considerable percentages (46.15 per cent) of respondents have opined that they are satisfied with the planning process at the state level only 'to some extent'. About one-third (30.77 per cent) respondents believed that the planning process at the state level is 'not at all' satisfactory. So far as the responses at the district level are concerned, more than half (53.85 per cent) respondents felt that the planning process at the district level is satisfactory only 'to some extent'. However, the percentage of dissatisfaction at the district level was rather low (15.38 per cent). The extent of satisfaction of the respondents varies considerably in responses could be for various reason which will probe at a later stage.

As we have reported earlier that the decentralised planning process is a participative process. Unless people effectively participate in the planning process at different levels, the purpose of decentralised planning may not be achieved. With this in view, the respondents were asked to express whether they have ever been involved in the planning process. The responses so received are presented in the Table 2 below :

Table. 2. Involvement in the Planning Process

Responses	*District*	
	Percentage of Bareilly	*Percentage of Gorakhpur*
Yes	87.50	38.46
No	12.50	61.54
Total	**100.00**	**100.00**

The variation in responses regarding involvement in the planning process can be clearly seen in the figures given in the table above. It is interesting to note that a very large percentage (87.50) of respondent in Bareilly district have opined positively towards their involvement in the planning process. However, the percentage of respondents in Gorakhpur districts it is low (38.46) as compared to Bareilly.

In case of Gorakhpur a considerable percentage of respondents (61.54) reported that they had no involvement in the planning process. One interpretation of this data could be that Bareilly being better in terms of development as compared to Gorakhpur, this gets reflected in the involvement of the non-officials in the planning process.

The success of planning has generally remained a debatable question. The journey of planned development started way back in the 50's which is still continuing. Moreover, there is no dearth of literature on various aspects of planning in India either. The people in power have their own views on the success of planning. However, we wanted to know from the respondents in the district as to how far they feel satisfied with planning as such. The responses received are given in the Table 3 below:

Table 3. How far Planning is Successful

Extent	*Percentage of Bareilly*	*Percentage of Gorakhpur*
To a large extent	12.50	23.08
To some extent	50.50	61.54
Not at all	37.50	15.38
Total	**100.00**	**100.00**

The respondents have differed in two districts regarding the success of planning. Fifty per cent respondents in Bareilly have opined that planning is successful only 'to some extent'. The percentage of respondent in Gorakhpur who opined that planning is successful 'to some extent' is higher (61.54 per cent). It can safely be argued that extent of satisfaction with planning in both the districts is only to some extent. It is interesting to note that in Bareilly the dissatisfaction with planning is considerable (37.50 per cent). The response category of 'to a large extent' is again low (12.50 per cent) in Bareilly though it is slightly higher (23.08 per cent) in Gorakhpur. It can thus be seen that planning still desires a lot in order to be largely a success story.

There are a number of organisations which are associated with the planning process at different levels. We wanted to assess the awareness level of the non-official respondents about these organisations. It is obvious if these non-officials are considerably aware their participation and involvement will show a positive trend. In view of this, the participants were asked to give their opinion about the organisation involved in the planning process. The responses received are being presented in the Table 4 below.

Table 4. Organisation Involved in the Planning Process

Organisation	*Bareilly*		*Gorakhpur*	
	State Level	*District Level*	*State Level*	*District Level*
State Planning Board	12.50	0.00	30.77	0.00
Municipal Corporation	0.00	12.50	0.00	15.39
DVDA	0.00	0.00	0.00	7.69
DPC	0.00	25.00	0.00	30.77
PWD	12.50	50.00	15.38	7.69
Zila Panchayat	0.00	0.00	0.00	15.39
No Response	75.00	12.50	53.85	23.07
Total	**100.00**	**100.00**	**100.00**	**100.00**

The percentage in the table above provides interesting indications so far as the awareness about the organisation involved in the planning process. In the planning process at the state level, the State Planning Board is the main and important organisation. But the awareness percentage of the non-official about this body is indeed reflects the lack of knowledge of these respondents. Even the awareness about the District Planning Committee is not very encouraging. It again shows the lack of awareness of the non-official respondents about the role of the DPC in the planning process.

Another-alarming information shows that there is no involvement of the Zila Panchayats in the planning process. Not a single respondent opined that these organisations are involved in the planning process. However, quite a few percentages of respondents opined in favour of PWD for their own reasons. Another alarming fact reflected by the percentage in the table above is that a large percentage (75 per cent) in Bareilly, and 53 per cent in Gorakhpur respondents gave no response. It appears that such a large percentage of respondents remain un-informed about the organisation involved in the planning process which does not speak well any way.

We are well aware that the country experimented with different strategies for planned development in its journey towards growth and development. Different people hold different views so far as the effectiveness of these strategies are concerned. We wanted to assess the opinion of the non-official respondents towards this question. They were, therefore, asked to respond to the query as to how far they think that the planning strategies have been able to address development adequately. The responses so received are given in the Table 5 below.

Table 5. Adequacy of Planning Strategies for Development

Extent	*Percentage of Bareilly*	*Percentage of Gorakhpur*
To a large extent	0.00	23.07
To some extent	75.00	69.23
Not at all	The basic premise of decentralised planning and its evolution 25.00	7.70
Total	**100.00**	**100.00**

As the percentages in the table show, majority of the respondents (75 per cent) in Bareilly and (69.23 per cent) in Gorakhpur opined that the planning strategies followed could address development only 'to some extent'. The percentage of response in 'not at all' category in Bareilly is 25 per cent whereas for Gorakhpur it is only 7.70 per cent which is a significant variation. It may be pointed here that district Gorakhpur is in the backward region of the State and it continues to be so. Even then the figures show slightly different picture as compared to Bareilly which is rated as developed.

There could be little difference of opinion that poverty and unemployment continues to be foremost concerns of the Government of the day. We observe considerable attention being paid by successive governments over the years to tackle poverty and unemployment the two major problems confronting rural India. During the course of our study, we also wanted to assess from the non-official respondents as to what is their opinion. They were therefore, asked to give their opinion as to how far they think that planning has been able to tackle poverty and unemployment. Their response is being presented in the Table 6 below.

Table 6. Ability of Planning to Tackle Poverty and Unemployment

Extent	*Percentage of Bareilly*	*Percentage of Gorakhpur*
To a large extent	0.00	0.00
To some extent	75.00	84.62
Not at all	25.00	15.38
Total	**100.00**	**100.00**

The percentages given in the table above of the responses received give a clear indication that the ability of planning to tackle poverty and unemployment has succeeded only 'to some extent'. The majority of the respondents in Bareilly (75 per cent) and (84 per cent) in Gorakhpur have opined in that category of response. It may be pertinent here to note that a substantial percentage of respondents felt that it has 'not at all' been able to tackle the poverty and unemployment problems facing rural India.

In the planning process the Panchayati Raj institutions are supposed to play a significant role in addressing the issues of the public. Ever since these institutions came into existence a lot was expected of them. In between several reform measures have also been affected to improve efficiency and effectiveness of these bodies. In view of these circumstances we wanted to ascertain from the non-official respondents as to how far they think that Panchayati Raj institutions have been able to effectively deal with issues of public importance. The responses are being given in Table 7 below.

Table 7. Effectiveness of Panchayati Raj Institution in dealing Public Issues

Extent	*Percentage of Bareilly*	*Percentage of Gorakhpur*
To a large extent	12.50	15.38
To some extent	75.00	69.24
Not at all	12.50	15.38
Total	**100.00**	**100.00**

In case of Panchayati Raj institutions the response pattern shows general satisfaction only 'to some extent'. It only goes to suggest that in spite of reforms the Panchayati Raj institutions have not been able to get satisfaction 'to a large extent'. There is still a good percentage which is 'not at all' satisfied. It suggests that there is still need for improvement.

With the inauguration of Integrated Rural Development Programme (IRDP) during the Sixth Plan period a simultaneous creation of District Rural Development Agency (DRDA) took place to specifically look after the newly launched poverty alleviation program. In a sense it was a departure from the earlier strategies adopted for rural development. In view of this we wanted to ascertain as to whether the DRDA has been effective in tackling the issues connected with rural development. The non-official respondents were thus, asked to give their opinion on this question. Their opinion is being presented in the table below.

Table 8. Effectiveness of DRDA in Tackling in Issues of Rural Development

Extent	*Percentage of Bareilly*	*Percentage of Gorakhpur*
To a large extent	25.00	7.69
To some extent	62.50	76.92
Not at all	12.50	15.39
Total	**100.00**	**100.00**

The response patterns to this query shows that the respondents seem to be satisfied only 'to some extent'. More than half of the respondents in both selected districts have opined that their satisfaction is only to some extent. The satisfaction category of 'large extent' is reported at 25 per cent in Bareilly and only 7.69 at Gorakhpur.

Decentralised Planning

We have already covered various issues connected with decentralised planning in earlier chapter. It is only pertinent to recollect that decentralised planning constitutes an important component and a strategy for rural development sector. In view of the importance of decentralised planning, we wanted to ascertain from the non-official respondents as to how far in their opinion decentralised planning model is a realistic model for the achievement of adequate development in the rural sector. Their responses are given in the Table 9 below.

Table 9. Decentralised Planning in Realistic Model

Extent	*Percentage of Bareilly*	*Percentage of Gorakhpur*
To a large extent	37.50	30.77
To some extent	25.00	38.76
Not at all	37.50	30.77
Total	**100.00**	**100.00**

The percentage given in the table shows a mixed response pattern. It is interesting to note that the non-official respondents in both the selected districts have given similar weightage 'to a large extent' satisfaction and to 'not at all', though the percentages slightly vary. It is 37.50 per cent for Bareilly whereas for Gorakhpur it is 30.77. It is, therefore, difficult to draw any realistic conclusion from these opinions. Also the percentage of response in 'to some extent' is only 25 per cent in Bareilly whereas it is 38.76 per cent for Gorakhpur.

The percentages in the above table do indicate that quite considerable number feel that the decentralised planning model is not a realistic model, though they have not been able to substantiate their opinion effectively.

The above observation gets corroborated when the non-official respondents were asked to tell whether they have an idea as to since when the decentralised planning model has been there in their districts. We give their responses in the Table 10 given below.

Table 10. Since When the Decentralised Planning Model

Period in years	*Percentage of Bareilly*	*Percentage of Gorakhpur*
Up to 2	62.50	23.08
10 to 20	Nil	38.46
No idea	37.50	38.46
Total	**100.00**	**100.00**

The percentage given in the table above provides interesting information about the level of awareness of the non-officials who are concerned with the decentralised planning model. In Bareilly district 62.50 per cent non-official respondents have opined that decentralised planning model was in existence only for the last two years. In Gorakhpur, the percentage is low but it is also significant that 23.08 per cent non-official respondents opted for 'up to two years' opinion. This could be seen as an indicator of the status or decentralised planning model in the State. Further interesting data shows that in both the selected districts about 38 per cent of the non-official respondents said that they have 'no idea' as to when the decentralised planning model started. This does not present any positive picture so far as the decentralised planning model of rural development in the State is concerned.

Panchayati Raj institutions were considered part of the process of decentralised planning from the beginning itself. Over the years they have evolved as an important segment of governance in the rural sector. In view of their importance in the overall scenario, we wanted to ascertain from the non-official respondents as to how far in their opinion the Panchayati Raj system has been effective in achieving the desired objectives in their respective districts. The response so received is given in the table below.

Table 11. Effectiveness of Panchayati Raj System

Extent	*Percentage of Bareilly*	*Percentage of Gorakhpur*
To a large extent	12.50	23.08
To some extent	87.50	61.54
Not at all	Nil	15.38
Total	**100.00**	**100.00**

It can be seen from the percentages given in the table above that the situation is not very encouraging. Most of the responses are in the category of 'to some extent' only. The response category of 'to large extent' does not provide any large number as in Bareilly it is only 12.50 and in Gorakhpur slightly higher to 23.08 per cent.

A lot was expected after the 73rd and 74th Constitutional Amendment Acts of 1992, so far as the organisational structure and the working of Local Government Institution - both rural and urban were concerned. It was thought that these Amendments will provide Constitutional status along with adequate powers and responsibilities to meet their Constitutional obligation. In the context of decentralised planning too they had their role in planning process. In view of their importance we wanted to know from the non-official respondents as to how far these Amendments have made an impact on the planning process. Their opinion is given in the Table 12 below.

Table 12. Impact of 73rd and 74th Constitutional Amendments in Planning Process

Extent	*Percentage of Bareilly*	*Percentage of Gorakhpur*
To a large extent	12.50	38.46
To some extent	87.50	30.77
Not at all	Nil	30.77
Total	**100.00**	**100.00**

The percentages given in the above table shows drastically different response pattern. In Bareilly, the non-official respondents have overwhelmingly (87.50) opined that the impact of these Constitutional Amendments has only been marginal as they opted for 'to some extent' response option. None of the respondents opined negatively. The responses for the Gorakhpur district are quite different as compared to Bareilly. Here about 38.46 per cent of the non-official respondents opined that these Amendments have affected the planning process in the district 'to a large extent'. On the contrary considerable percentage of non-official respondents with identical percentage of 30.77 has opted for two different options viz. One says 'to some extent' while the other opines 'not at all'. It can be argued here that there are a considerable percentage of respondents who feel that there is little impact of these Amendments on the planning process in the district.

We have noticed earlier about the decentralised planning model where the respondents gave their opinion as to whether decentralised planning model is a realistic model. We also wanted to know from the non-official respondents about the appropriateness of the decentralised planning model. They responded to question and their responses are given in the Table 13 below:

Table 13. Decentralised Planning Model an Appropriate Model for Development

Extent	*Percentage of Bareilly*	*Percentage of Gorakhpur*
To a large extent	12.50	38.46
To some extent	75.00	53.86
Not at all	12.50	7.69
Total	**100.00**	**100.00**

It can be seen from the percentages given in the table above that majority of respondents in both the selected districts have opined positively in favour of decentralised planning model as an appropriate model of development. Only a negligible percentage in both the districts — 12.50 in Bareilly and 7.65 in Gorakhpur have given a negative thought to decentralised planning model as an appropriate model of development.

The District Planning Committee had been assigned a specific task under the Constitution in the context of decentralised planning. All the State governments were under obligation to constitute the District Planning Committee in their respective States as stipulated by the Constitution. The information available through secondary sources showed that different States have taken different issues on the formation of the DPCs and the same got delayed for one reason or other. In case of Uttar Pradesh, we wanted to ascertain from the non-officials whether they are aware of this timing of the constitution of the DPCs in their own district. The information received through the questionnaire shows that quite a few of them were not aware as they had no idea. Some of them, who reported of knowing about the Constitution did not know correctly as to when the DPC was constituted in their respective districts. It only shows the seriousness of the non-officials connected with the decentralised planning process. We further probed and asked their opinion on whether there was delay in constituting the DPC. They agreed that there was delay in constituting the DPC. In Bareilly, every non-official participants (100 per cent) was of the opinion that there was delay in constituting the DPC. In Gorakhpur, this figure is 76.92 per cent.

The respondents were conscious of the fact that there was delay in constituting the DPC in the district. We therefore, wanted to probe further to ascertain the reasons for the delay. The responses received are given in the Table 14 below.

Table 14. Reasons for Delay in Constituting the DPC

Extent	*Percentage of Bareilly*	*Percentage of Gorakhpur*
Lack of political will	75.00	46.15
Bureaucracy	25.00	38.46
No Idea	Nil	15.39
Total	**100.00**	**100.00**

The respondents were given two major options viz., the lack of political will and the bureaucracy. The third option was for those who had no idea. It is interesting to note that in both the selected districts the non-official respondents opined that the delay in constituting the DPC was 'lack of political will'. A considerable percentage of respondents in both the districts, viz., 32.50 per cent in Bareilly and 38.46 per cent in Gorakhpur, held bureaucracy responsible for the delay in constituting the DPC.

After the District Planning Committees were constituted it was imperative to know as to when these bodies started functioning. The non-officials were thus asked to give their opinion about the timing of the functioning of the DPC in their respective districts. Their opinion is given in the Table 15 below.

Table 15. Starting Period of Functioning of the DPC

Extent	*Percentage of Bareilly*	*Percentage of Gorakhpur*
Within one year	12.50	30.76
Within two years	87.50	30.76
No Idea	Nil	38.48
Total	**100.00**	**100.00**

The opinions of non-official respondents vary so far as the starting timing of the DPC in the district is concerned. Although the DPC were constituted in the State by the Government Order but the districts took their own time in formally constituting and making the DPCs functional. The figures given in the table above shows that in Bareilly majority of the non-official respondents (87.50 per cent) opined that the DPC started working within two years of its constitution. However, in Gorakhpur the percentage for the same period is only 30.76. Also, a considerable percentage (38.48) in Gorakhpur said that they had no idea as to when the DPC started functioning.

After recording their opinion about the starting time of the DPC, we wanted to know from them as to how many of them are member of the District Planning Committee. The responses so received are given in the Table 16 below.

Table 16. Whether Member of District Planning Committee

Response	*Percentage of Bareilly*	*Percentage of Gorakhpur*
Yes	75.00	38.46
No	25.00	61.54
Total	**100.00**	**100.00**

It can be seen from the figure given in the above table that in Bareilly three-fourth of the respondents were members of the DPC while the remaining one-fourth were not the members of the DPC. The situation for Gorakhpur is somewhat different where about 38 per cent were members and the remaining about 38 per cent were members and the remaining about 62 per cent were not the members of the DPC.

After getting the information about the membership of the DPC, the respondents were asked to give their opinion about the performance of the DPC. We have already noted that there was delay in constituting the DPC. There was lack of political as well as the bureaucratic hurdles in constituting the DPC in the State. We now wanted to know from the non-official respondents as to how far the DPC has been able to perform their responsibilities satisfactorily. The responses received are given in the Table 17 below.

Table 17. Satisfaction about Performance of the DPC

Extent	*Percentage of Bareilly*	*Percentage of Gorakhpur*
To a large extent	Nil	15.38
To some extent	12.50	61.54
Not at all	87.50	23.08
Total	100.00	100.00

The percentages given in the table above does not give us encouraging statistics about the performance of the DPC, in UP.

In Bareilly district none of the respondents reported 'to a large extent' category only a negligible percentage (12.50) opined 'to some extent' category response. It appears to be a dismal feeling as 87.50 per cent non-official respondents opined that the performance of the DPC is not at all satisfactory. This is the situation reported for Bareilly district. The situation in Gorakhpur seems to be slightly better where 61.54 per cent respondents expressed that they are satisfied 'to some extent' with the performance of the DPC. However, about one-fourth of the respondents were also reported that they are 'not at all' satisfied with the working of the DPC in the district.

The planning process is a time-bound process. Since the DPCs have a definite role in decentralised planning as they are supposed to consolidate the district plan, the whole process has to be time-bound. In view of this, we wanted to know from the non-official respondents whether the DPC has been able to complete the exercise in time. The responses received are given in the Table 18 below.

Table 18. Formulating the Plan in Time

Response	*Percentage of Bareilly*	*Percentage of Gorakhpur*
To a large extent	Nil	7.70
To some extent	75.00	61.54
Not at all	25.00	30.76
Total	**100.00**	**100.00**

The above table clearly indicates that the non-official respondents in both the districts opined that only 'to some extent' plans were completed in time. A considerable percentage of respondents in both the districts viz., 25 per cent in Bareilly and 30.76 per cent in Gorakhpur felt that 'not at all' is the appropriate category of response. It can be observed that delays must have occurred in the process which made the respondents to react in this manner.

An important component of planning exercise is the fixation of priorities. The planning process includes various levels at which the plans are being prepared wherein the priorities are supposed to be fixed. Priorities for different districts in the State may not be the same as their needs and resource base would vary. The State will have its own priorities taking into account the general need and the resources available. In view of this, we wanted to know from the non-official respondents whether priorities for the State and the district vary or it is uniform for the State as well as districts. The responses received are given in the Table 19 below.

Table 19. Nature of the Plan Priorities for the State and Districts

Response	*Percentage of Bareilly*	*Percentage of Gorakhpur*
Uniform	87.50	46.15
Vary	12.50	53.85
Total	**100.00**	**100.00**

It can well be seen from the figures given in the table above that there is variation in response pattern of the two selected districts. In Bareilly district about 88 per cent of the respondents have said that it is uniform for the State as well as the district. Only a thin percentage of about 12 felt that the priority for the State and the district vary, they are not uniform. However, the respondents in Gorakhpur have responded differently to this question. More than half of the respondents (53.85 per cent) opined that the priorities for the State and the district vary whereas about 46 per cent of the respondents opined that it is uniform. It is also noteworthy that the percentage difference between the two responses is not much.

As we have already noted at several places in the earlier pages that the decentralised planning process is a participative planning process and covers the area of the district and below. In that sense, therefore, the priorities of the State in general and the districts across the State may not be the same. Of course, there could be plan priorities fixed by the State for the State and within those the district would like to decide about their own priorities depending upon their need and the resource base. In this context, therefore, the data provided by the non-official respondent become an important indicator for further probing and analysis.

The participants were asked to give their opinion on yet another question. We wanted to know from the participants as to how far the priorities fixed by the DPC are as per the needs of the area. This was considered important as the district plan in order to be realistic has to base itself on the needs of the area. The responses received are given in the Table 20 below.

Table 20. Priorities Fixed by the DPC as per the Need

Response	*Percentage of Bareilly*	*Percentage of Gorakhpur*
To a large extent	12.50	15.38
To some extent	75.00	61.54
Not at all	12.00	23.08
Total	**100.00**	**100.00**

The figures given in the table above suggests that the non-official respondents in both the selected districts have predominantly opined that the DPC decides about the priorities of the plan as per need only 'to some extent'. In Bareilly (75 per cent) and in Gorakhpur about 61 per cent respondents have expressed their opinion in 'to some extent' category. The other two opinions did not receive high priority in the opinion of the respondent in Bareilly. However, in Gorakhpur about one-fourth of the respondent expressed that the DPC 'not at all' fixes the priorities according to the need of the district.

The planning exercise does require knowledge and skill by the planner in order to prepare a proper plan. Lack of knowledge and skill by the members who are responsible for plan preparation or for consolidation or plan will not help the proper plan formulation. In view of this we wanted to ascertain from the non-official respondents as to how far the members of the DPC are knowledgeable enough for the task in hand. Their responses are given in the Table 21 below.

Table 21. DPC Members are Knowledgeable Enough for Task in Hand

Extent	*Percentage of Bareilly*	*Percentage of Gorakhpur*
To a large extent	Nil	7.69
To some extent	87.50	53.85
Not at all	12.50	38.46
Total	**100.00**	**100.00**

The figures given in the table above for the two selected districts varies. In Bareilly, an overwhelming percentage of respondents (87.50) have expressed that only 'to some extent' the members of the DPC are knowledgeable enough for the task in hand. Interestingly, none of the respondents is reported in the response category of 'to a large extent', though a negligible percentage of respondents (12.50) are shown in the response category 'not at all, the response percentage for Gorakhpur slightly varies from that of Bareilly. Here, one can see that more than half of the non-official respondents (53.85) have opined that the DPC members have only 'to some extent' the knowledge for the task in hand. A considerable percentage of the respondents (38.46 per cent) have expressed that the DPC members, 'not al all' possess the knowledge for the task they have in their hands. It can be observed here that these figures do not speak well of the role and responsibilities of the District Planning Committees in the State.

We are aware that in the State as well as in other States across the country different strategies have been adopted for planning and development in different Plan periods. Taking this into account we wanted to know from the non-official respondents whether the strategies followed earlier were affective for achieving development or the strategies adopted in present times are effective in achieving development. Their responses are being given in the table below.

Table 22. Effectiveness of Strategies — The Earlier and Present for Development

Response Extent	*Percentage of Bareilly*		*Percentage of Gorakhpur*	
	Earlier	*Present*	*Earlier*	*Present*
To a large extent	Nil	37.50	7.70	58.46
To some extent	62.50	62.50	64.54	53.85
Not at all	37.50	Nil	30.76	7.69
Total	**100.00**	**100.00**	**100.00**	**100.00**

The district-wise responses given in the table above gives a mixed response pattern. The two districts provide different response patterns. In Bareilly, no response is reported in response category 'to a large extent' for the 'earlier' strategies but 37.50 per cent opined in this response category for the 'present' strategy. However, the response percentage is identically divided in response category of 'to some extent' for both option of strategies, viz., the earlier and the present. It is significant to note that the respondents in Bareilly have clearly indicated that 'earlier' strategy was 'not at all' effective for achieving development. The response pattern for Gorakhpur district is slightly different from that of Bareilly district. It is significant to note that the non-official respondents in Gorakhpur have opined (61.54 per cent) 'to some extent' for the 'earlier' strategy in order to achieve effective development which is almost the same percentage reported for Bareilly in that response category. But in Gorakhpur the choice of 'present' strategy is 'to some extent' response category is 53.85 per cent which is slightly lower than the option 'earlier'. A contrasting situation is seen when the respondents opted (30.76 per cent) 'not at all' option for the 'earlier' strategy. The overall indication of the figure given in the table above can be drawn that the 'present' strategy should be given primacy over the 'earlier' one for achieving effective development.

The Institutional Set up and Networking

Over the years, we observe that these have been several agencies operating at district level for the purpose of development in the area. Even in the decentralised planning there are multiple agencies involved. We therefore, wanted to ascertain from the non-official respondents as to how far they agree with this institutional arrangement for decentralised planning. Their responses are given in the Table 23 below.

Table. 23. Agree about Multiple Agencies for Decentralised Planning

Extent	*Percentage of Bareilly*	*Percentage of Gorakhpur*
To a large extent	75.00	30.77
To some extent	25.00	53.85
Not at all	Nil	15.38
Total	**100.00**	**100.00**

The figures given in the table above provides a variation in response pattern of the two selected districts. In Bareilly, 75 per cent of the non-official respondents opined that there are multiple agencies for decentralised planning in the district. Only one-fourth of the respondents expressed only 'to some extent' response option. The responses of the non-official respondent in Gorakhpur show a slight variation in this option. Here only 30.77 per cent agreed 'to a large extent' that there are multiple agencies for decentralised planning in the district. However, more than half (53.85 per cent) opined in favour of 'to some extent' response option. We can well observe on the basis of these figures that the respondents have by and large, agreed that there are multiple agencies for decentralised planning in the district. This will be another question as to whether this multiplicity has helped the decentralised planning process or not.

In a subsequent query, we wanted to know from the non-official respondents about the various agencies involved in the decentralised planning process. The respondents were provided with the names of these agencies and they were asked to tick their option. The responses received are given in the table below.

Table 24. Agencies Involved in Decentralised Planning

Agencies	*Percentage of Bareilly*	*Percentage of Gorakhpur*
D.R.D.A.	Nil	15.38
Panchayati Raj Institution	50.00	15.38
District Administration	Nil	Nil
DRDA and PRIs	12.50	15.38
PRIs and District Administration	Nil	7.70
DRDA, PRI and DA	Nil	30.78
PRI, DA and Govt. Department	12.50	15.38
Govt. Department and DRDA	25.00	Nil
Total	**100.00**	**100.00**

The responses recorded in the table above indicate that these responses are multiple responses, though some answers are for one agency but majority of the responses are multiple response. It can be derived from the responses given in the table above that there is more than one agency involved in the decentralised planning process. The non-official respondent in both the districts have identified the Panchayati Raj Institution (PRI) as the major agency involved in the decentralised planning process. The other institutions which figure in the decentralised planning process are the DRDA, District Administration and the Government Departments.

The non-official respondents were subsequently asked about the impact of the multiple agencies on the decentralised planning process as we wanted to know whether the multiplicity of agencies have affected the decentralised planning process. In view of this, they were asked to give their opinion on this question. Their responses are given in the table below.

Table 25. Multiplicity of Agencies Affected Decentralised Planning Process

Extent	*Percentage of Bareilly*	*Percentage of Gorakhpur*
To a large extent	62.50	15.38
To some extent	37.50	53.85
Not at all	Nil	30.77
Total	**100.00**	**100.00**

It can well be interpreted from the data presented in the above table that an almost absolute majority of respondents in both the selected districts have opined that the multiplicity of agencies has definitely affected the decentralised planning process. At the same time, there is variation in response pattern in both the districts while in Bareilly none of the respondents felt that it has affected the decentralised planning process where as in Gorakhpur almost more than one-fourth (30.77 per cent) opined that it did not affect the planning process at all.

In the decentralised planning process we have identified quite a few institutions which are involved in the activity. A proper networking of these institutions is considered important for proper and effective decentralised planning process. In view of the importance of this institutional networking, we wanted to know from the non-official respondents as to how far this institutional networking has been able to address the issue adequately. Their opinion is being presented in the Table 26 below.

Table 26. Ability of How Institutions to Deal with Issue Adequately

Extent	*Percentage of Bareilly*	*Percentage of Gorakhpur*
To a large extent	37.50	15.38
To some extent	37.50	61.54
Not at all	25.00	23.08
Total	**100.00**	**100.00**

The figures given in the above table give different response pattern for the two selected districts. In Bareilly, majority of the non-official respondents felt that the non-institutions have been able to address the issue adequately, even though about one-fourth of the respondents expressed an altogether different opinion. So far as respondents in Gorakhpur are concerned majority of them expressed that only 'to some extent' the new institutions were able to address the issues adequately. About one-fourth respondents (23.08 per cent) opined that the new institutions were 'not at all' able to address the issues adequately.

We have expressed earlier in the report that the Panchayati Raj Institutions (PRIs) occupy a significant role in the decentralised planning process. This has been the general opinion expressed by the people, who are supposed to be informed about the system. Keeping this in view, we wanted to ascertain from the non-official respondents again as to whether in their opinion the Panchayati Raj institutions have helped the cause of decentralised planning. The opinion gathered from the respondents is given in Table 27 as under.

Table 27. Involvement of the PRIs Has Helped the Cause of Decentralised Planning

Extent	*Percentage of Bareilly*	*Percentage of Gorakhpur*
To a large extent	25.00	15.38
To some extent	75.00	69.24
Not at all	Nil	15.38
Total	**100.00**	**100.00**

The figures given in the table show the percentage variations of the respondents in the two selected districts. So far as the response category of 'to some extent' is concerned, there is not much variation in the responses given by the respondents in the two districts as it is 75 per cent in Bareilly, and 69.24 in Gorakhpur, both are high percentage responses. However, there is variation in other two categories of this response. Whereas in Bareilly one-fourth of the respondents opined for 'to a great extent' category, the figure for Gorakhpur in the same category response is only 15.38 per cent. Further, in 'not at all' category response, in Bareilly none of the respondents opted for this category while in Gorakhpur about 15.38 per cent respondents opined for this category response.

Another important component in any planning exercise is the problem of co-ordination. There are several agencies involved at different levels therefore, for proper planning effective co-ordination becomes a necessary ingredient. In view of the importance of co-ordination we wanted to know from the non-official respondents as to how far they feel satisfied with co-ordination of different agencies for the purpose of decentralised planning. Their responses are given in the Table 28 below.

Table 28. Satisfaction About Coordination among Various Agencies

Extent	*Bareilly per cent*	*Gorakhpur per cent*
To a large extent	Nil	Nil
To some extent	87.50	46.15
Not at all	12.50	53.85
Total	**100.00**	**100.00**

There is no problem in comprehending that lack of co-ordination will definitely affect the planning process adequately. The figures given in the above table reveal that no respondents is reported to be satisfied 'to a large extent' in both the selected districts. The degree of satisfaction however, varies in the two selected districts for other two-response option. In Bareilly, an overwhelming majority (87.50 per cent) of the respondents opined that they are satisfied only 'to some extent' and another meager (12.50 per cent) reported that they are 'not at all' satisfied. In Gorakhpur, response category of 'to some extent' is reported at 46.65 per cent which is lower than 'not at all' category which is 53.85 per cent. It gives an important indication that the non-official respondents in the district are not satisfied with the level of co-ordination in the decentralised planning process. It can be inferred that this might have affected the planning process to some extent.

It is considered significant from the achievement point of view that those involved should take their job rather seriously otherwise the desired objective will be difficult to achieve. In view of this, we wanted to know as to how far the institutions involved have taken their job seriously. The responses received are given in the Table 29 below.

Table 29. Institutions Involved have Taken their Job Seriously

Extent	*Percentage of Bareilly*	*Percentage of Gorakhpur*
To a large extent	Nil	7.69
To some extent	87.50	84.62
Not at all	12.50	7.69
Total	**100.00**	**100.00**

A glance at the table above shows that there is not much variation in the response pattern of the two districts. However, in the response category 'to a large extent' no respondents in Bareilly district opted for this option although in Gorakhpur 7.69 per cent respondents did report in two response categories. In the response category of 'to some extent' there is not much variation could be seen as 87.50 in Bareilly and 84.62 per cent in Gorakhpur expressed their opinion in this response category. In the response category of 'not at all' there appears to be little variation in responses opted for in the two districts. In Bareilly, 12.50 per cent respondents opted for this response category while in Gorakhpur only 7.69 reported in this category. An overall assessment could be that predominantly respondents favoured the 'to some extent' category showing that there is lot of scope for improvement. The institutions involved need to look again their job profile and take the same a bit seriously to achieve the desired results.

Another important input for an effective and efficient decentralised planning in concerned with the skills required for the jobs. Planning does require some skill in order to formulate a proper plan. In view of the importance of this we wanted to know from the non-official respondents as to how far in their opinion the institutions involved in plan formulation had required skill. Their responses are given in the Table 30 under.

Table 30. Institutions having Required Skill

Extent	*Percentage of Bareilly*	*Percentage of Gorakhpur*
To a large extent	Nil	Nil
To some extent	87.50	92.31
Not at all	12.50	7.69
Total	**100.00**	**100.00**

The figures in the above table clearly indicate that the institutes involved in the decentralised planning process had the required skill but only 'to some extent'. It is important to note that not a single respondent opined that these institutions had the required skill 'to a large extent'. Moreover, some percentages are also reported in both the districts in 'not at all' response category. One inference that can safely be drawn out of these responses is that there is much scope for improvement in the area of skill required for decentralised planning process.

There is no denying the fact that infrastructure facilities do have a contribution to make in achieving the goals of decentralised planning. In the absence of proper infrastructural facilities it would

Table 31. Satisfaction with Infrastructural Facilities for Planning

Extent	*Percentage of Bareilly*	*Percentage of Gorakhpur*
To a large extent	Nil	23.08
To some extent	87.50	53.84
Not at all	12.50	23.08
Total	**100.00**	**100.00**

difficult to achieve the desired objectives. In view of the importance we wanted to know from the respondents as to how far they are satisfied with the infrastructural facilities provided for the decentralised planning in his district. Their responses are given in the Table 31.

The figures given in the table above clearly indicate the response pattern of the non-official respondents in the two selected districts which shows the variation. In Bareilly, the dominant percentage of respondents (87.50 per cent) opined for 'to some extent' response option whereas none is reported in 'to a large extent' category response. On the contrary, 12.50 per cent respondents opined for 'not at all' response category. However, in Gorakhpur we notice a slight change in percentages of the responses given. Here about one-fourth of the respondents did favour the 'to a large extent' response option, though almost identical percentage of respondents opted for 'not at all' response option. About half of the respondents opined that they are 'to some extent' satisfied with the infrastructural facilities provided for the decentralised planning in the district. This again goes to suggest that there is scope for improvement and the authorities concerned may like to look into this aspect.

The Planning Process: The Official Response

In order to get first hand information from the field we administered two sets of questionnaire—one on the non-official and the other on officials. We have briefly covered the analysis based on the information received from the non-official. In this section, we propose to take up the analysis based on the information received through the questionnaire on the official. Initially, we wanted to know from the official about their experience in the field planning. The respondents were asked to tell since how long they have been associated with the planning process. Their responses are presented in the Table 32 below.

Table 32. Since how Long Associated with the Planning Process

Term	*Percentage of Bareilly*	*Percentage of Gorakhpur*
Less than 5 Years	16.67	14.29
5 to 10 Years	16.67	28.57
10 to 15 Years	50.00	28.57
More than 15 Years	16.66	28.57
Total	**100.00**	**100.00**

The figures given above indicate that about one third of the respondents in Bareilly district have been associated with the planning process up to 10 years. About half of the respondents expressed that they have been associated with the planning process for 10 to 15 years. It shows that the officials in Bareilly district had a long experience so far as the planning process is concerned. In Gorakhpur district the last three options give an identical percentage of 28.57 per cent which goes to suggest that in Gorakhpur district also the officials had a long experience with the planning process.

Since planning has long been in existence, we wanted to know from the respondents as to how far they feel satisfied with the planning efforts made in the State. The responses received are given in table below.

Table 33. Satisfaction with Planning Efforts

Extent	*Percentage of Bareilly*	*Percentage of Gorakhpur*
To a large extent	16.67	28.57
To some extent	83.33	71.43
Not at all	Nil	Nil
Total	**100.00**	**100.00**

It can clearly be seen from the figures given in the table above that in both the selected districts the respondents overwhelmingly opined in favour of 'to some extent' response option. It is interesting to note that no respondent in either of the selected districts said that he is 'not at all' satisfied with the planning effort in the State.

In a subsequent query, we wanted to know from the official respondents as to which are the organisations responsible for preparing Five Year Plan at the State and at the district levels. Their responses are given in the Table 34 below.

Table 34. Organisations Responsible for Preparing Five Year Plan

Name of the Organisation	*Percentage of Bareilly*	*Percentage of Gorakhpur*
(A) State Level		
(i) State Planning Committee/Planning Deptt	83.33	71.43
(ii) No Idea	16.67	28.57
(B) District Level		
(i) DPC	66.66	85.71
(ii) Economic and Statistic Divisions	16.67	14.29
(iii) Nagar Nigam	16.76	Nil

The figures given in the table above about the organisations responsible for preparing five year plans the respondents in both the selected districts have given the names of such organisations from State as well as for the district. For the State majority of the respondents in both the selected districts have opined that it is the State Planning Board and the Planning Department of the Gorakhpur which generally prepares the five year plan. So far as the preparation of district plan is concerned, the respondents in both the selected districts have opined that it is the District Planning Committee which is preparing the district plan.

In order to achieve the desired objectives, the planning machinery at different levels has to be effective. We therefore, wanted to know from the officials as to what is their experience. They were asked to tell as to how far they think that the planning machinery at different levels is effective. Their responses are given in the table below.

Table. 35. Effectiveness of Planning Machinery at Different Levels

Extent	*Percentage of Bareilly*		*Percentage of Gorakhpur*	
	District	*State*	*State*	*District*
To a large extent	33.33	33.33	28.57	14.29
To some extent	66.67	66.67	71.43	85.71
Not at all	Nil	Nil	Nil	Nil
Total	**100.00**	**100.00**	**100.00**	**100.00**

The above table clearly indicates that the planning machinery at different levels has been effective. However, a considerable majority of official respondents have opined that the planning machinery has been effective. There are variations in percentage response in the two selected districts. In Bareilly about one third (33.33 per cent) respondents said that the planning machinery at both the levels has been effective. The response category of 'to some extent' recorded 66.67 for both, the State as well as the district. There was no response in the response category of 'not at all' in both the selected districts. In Gorakhpur, we observe variation in response percentages for the State and the district. The official respondents opined that at the State level (71.43 per cent) is effective 'to some extent' while the percentage from the district for the same category response is quite higher (85.71 per cent). One inference that can be drawn for the percentage reported here that the machinery for planning appear to be more effective at the district level than at the State level.

It is considered important that the people, who are associated with the planning process take their job rather seriously in order to make planning an effective tool of development. In view of this, we wanted to know the opinion of the officials as to how far they think that people associated with planning take their job seriously. Their responses are given in the Table 36 below.

Table 36. People Associated with Planning Take their Job Seriously

Extent	*Percentage of Bareilly*	*Percentage of Gorakhpur*
To a large extent	33.33	28.57
To some extent	66.67	71.43
Not at all	Nil	Nil
Total	**100.00**	**100.00**

It can clearly be seen from the figures given in the table above that there is little difference in the response pattern of the two districts selected for the purpose. In both the districts, the respondents have largely opted for 'to some extent' response pattern, though there is slight variation in percentages in both the districts. In the other response category of 'to a large extent', about one-third respondent in Bareilly opted for their response pattern whereas in Gorakhpur the percentage is only 28.57 per cent which is slightly lower. Interestingly, in the third category of the response option 'not at all' there is no response in this category meaning thereby that the respondents have not given any priority to this response option.

We have already discussed various issues connected with decentralisation in earlier chapter. However, we wanted to ascertain from the official respondents about the utility of the decentralised planning for development in general. In view of this, we asked the respondents as to how far they think that decentralisation is good for development. The responses received are presented as under in the Table 37.

Table 37. How Far Decentralisation is Good for Development

Extent	*Percentage of Bareilly*	*Percentage of Gorakhpur*
To a large extent	83.33	89.71
To some extent	16.67	14.29
Not at all	Nil	Nil
Total	**100.00**	**100.00**

The figures given in the table clearly indicate the opinion of the official respondents which seems to be almost unanimous that decentralisation is good for development. We can see that the respondents overwhelmingly opined that decentralisation is good for development. In Bareilly, 83.33 per cent of the respondents and in Gorakhpur 89.71 per cent of the respondents opined in favour of decentralisation. It clearly shows that the officials in both the districts are quite clear in their understanding about the role of decentralisation in the development process.

It is generally accepted that Panchayati Raj plays an important role in rural governance. It has significant contribution to make in the decentralised planning process. Ever since the acceptance of Balwant Rai Mehta Committee Report's recommendation by the Government the Panchayati Raj has been the main instrument of democratic decentralisation and governance in rural India. In view of the importance of Panchayati Raj institutions in general and their role in decentralised planning in particular, we just wanted to know from the official as to how far they are aware of their systems. We, thus asked them that if they are aware, since when the Panchayati Raj came into formal existence in the country. Their responses are given in Table 38 below.

Table 38. Since When Panchayati Raj Came into Existence

Year	*Percentage of Bareilly*	*Percentage of Gorakhpur*
1994	50.00	28.57
1989	Nil	28.57
1947	33.33	14.29
No Idea	16.67	28.57
Total	**100.00**	**100.00**

The figures given in the table above reveal interesting data. The respondents in the two selected districts provide varying response pattern. In Bareilly district half of the respondents opined that Panchayati Raj came into existence in the year 1994, therefore they are not acknowledging the existence of Panchayati Raj before that. It appears that they are attributing the existence of Panchayati Raj with the 73rd Constitutional Amendment Act, and subsequent amendments to the State laws. As against this about one-third of the respondents in the district opined that it came into existence in the year 1947. The officials in the State seem to be a bit confused with regard to Panchayati Raj. It is a fact that in U.P. Panchayat Raj

Act was passed in the year 1947 but it was not a Panchayati Raj as it only confined itself to the panchayats. The response given by the official for Gorakhpur district provides a different pattern. In Gorakhpur about 29 per cent respondents opined that Panchayati Raj came into existence in the year 1994. Almost similar percentage of the official expressed that it came into existence in the year 1989. Interestingly, a similar percentage of 28.57 had no idea as to when the Panchayati Raj came into existence. A very limited percentage of 14 per cent opined that it came into existence in the year 1947. The opinion provided by the official of Gorakhpur district is almost equally distributed among the three options and therefore, it can be argued that their information about the existence of Panchayati Raj is fairly vague which does not account well for the people who have themselves been associated with Panchayati Raj in one-way or the other.

Decentralised Planning Model

For an effective and efficient development particularly for the rural sector, there has almost been a continuous effort by the Government with variation during different plan periods. Moreover, we find a general agreement amongst the policy planner about the role of decentralised planning for development. Keeping in view the importance of decentralised planning for development we wanted to know from the official respondents as to how far they think that the decentralised planning model has been effective. Their responses are being presented in the Table 39 below.

Table 39. Effectiveness of Decentralised Planning Model

Extent	*Percentage of Bareilly*	*Percentage of Gorakhpur*
To a large extent	66.67	14.29
To some extent	33.33	57.14
Not at all	Nil	28.57
Total	**100.00**	**100.00**

There appears to be a general consensus amongst the official respondents of the selected districts that decentralised planning is an effective model for development. In Bareilly district about 77 per cent of the respondents opined that 'to a large extent' decentralised planning is an effective model whereas about one-third of the respondents felt that 'to some extent' it is an effective model for development. The opinion of the respondents in Gorakhpur district slightly varies as only 14 per cent of the respondents opted for 'to a large extent' option. The majority of the respondents thus opined that only 'to some extent' the decentralised planning is an effective model. However, about 28.57 per cent of the respondents said that it is not effective.

Since planning is a 'state' subject under the List of Subjects under the Constitution, we wanted to know from the officials whether they are well aware of the decentralised planning process in their State. They were asked to tell as to when the State accepted the decentralised planning model for development. Their responses are given in the Table 40 as under.

Table 40. Since When the State Accepted the Decentralised Planning Model

Extent	*Percentage of Bareilly*	*Percentage of Gorakhpur*
2007	50.00	Nil
2008	50.00	Nil
1993-94	Nil	57.14
1982-83	Nil	42.86
Total	**100.00**	**100.00**

The information level of the official of the two selected districts provides entirely contradictory information so far as the beginning of decentralised planning model in the State is concerned. In Bareilly, respondents are equally divided into two broad options which suggest that it began in the years 2007 and 2008. It appears that they are thinking of the steps taken after the constitution of the District Planning Committees in the State and not the steps taken before that. The respondents in Gorakhpur district have altogether different understanding of the starting of the decentralised planning model in the State. In Gorakhpur, majority of the respondents 57.14 per cent opined that it started in the year 1993-94 whereas 42.86 per cent opined that it started in the year 1982-83. It appears that the respondents in Gorakhpur feel that it started with the reform of 73rd and 74th Constitutional Amendments since they opted for that year. Again the respondents who opted for 1982-83 option may be thinking of the Sixth Plan period when steps were taken in this regard. In either of the district we think the respondents could not take the questions in the right perspective. It is a matter of concern that the official in both the district could not comprehend the question in the right perspective.

As expressed earlier, the Panchayati Raj system forms an important component in the decentralised planning process. It plays a significant role in governance in rural sector. In view of the importance of the Panchayati Raj system we wanted to ascertain from the officials as to what is their opinion about the system. How far they think the system has been successful. Their responses are given in the Table 41 below.

Table 41. How far the Panchayati Raj System has been Successful

Extent	*Percentage of Bareilly*	*Percentage of Gorakhpur*
To a large extent	50.00	14.29
To some extent	33.33	71.42
Not at all	16.67	14.29
Total	**100.00**	**100.00**

The figures given in the table above provides varying percentages for the two selected districts in the State. In Bareilly, half of the official respondents expressed that Panchayati Raj has been successful 'to a great extent'. This is a dominant opinion so far as the Panchayati Raj system is concerned. The other one-third of the official respondents opined that only 'to some extent' the Panchayati Raj system has been successful in the State. Although not a very significant percentage (16.67) said that Panchayati Raj has 'not at all' been successful. But the percentage for various response categories for Gorakhpur varies considerably from that of Bareilly. Only 14.29 per cent of the respondents in Gorakhpur opined in favour of 'to a large extent' response category. The majority of the respondents 71.42 favoured 'to some extent' response option to suggest that Panchayati Raj has not been that successful. Moreover, a small percentage 14.29 opted for 'not at all' response option suggesting that Panchayati Raj has not been successful.

The 73rd and 74th Constitutional Amendments have brought about changes in various spheres of governance in the local government sector — both the rural and the urban areas. It was considered to be the historic development in the field of local government in the sense of providing them the long sought after autonomy along with other important focusses. In view of the importance of these Amendments, we wanted to know from the official respondents as to how far these Amendments have made an impact on the planning process in their State. The responses received are presented in the Table 42 as under.

Table 42. Impact of Constitutional Amendment (73rd and 74th) on the Planning Process

Extent	*Percentage of Bareilly*	*Percentage of Gorakhpur*
To a large extent	83.33	28.57
To some extent	16.67	57.14
Not at all	Nil	14.29
Total	**100.00**	**100.00**

It can clearly be seen from the figures given in the table above that there is variation in response pattern of the officials of the two selected districts. In Bareilly district, an overwhelming majority (83.33 per cent) of the respondents expressed that the Constitutional Amendments had affected the planning process 'to a large extent'. The remaining 16.67 per cent respondents opted for 'to some extent' response option. In Gorakhpur, the response pattern provides a different response. In the response option of 'to some extent' majority of the respondents (57.14 per cent) opined that Amendments affected the planning process. About 29 per cent respondents expressed in favour of 'to a large extent' response option which is not much. Some 14 per cent respondents though said that there is almost no impact of this Amendment on the planning process. It can therefore be seen that perspective of the officials in the two selected districts varies.

After seeking the opinion of the respondents on the impact of the Constitutional Amendments on the planning process, we chose to question the officials on the decentralised planning model. As we have reported earlier in the report, the decentralised planning model has attracted the attention of this policy planner quite early in our planning effort for development. It is now generally an accepted model for development. In view of this, we wanted to ascertain from the official their view point as they are at the ground level. Their responses are presented in the Table 43 as under.

Table. 43. Decentralised Planning Model an Appropriate Model

Extent	*Percentage of Bareilly*	*Percentage of Gorakhpur*
To a large extent	66.67	42.86
To some extent	33.33	42.86
Not at all	Nil	14.28
Total	**100.00**	**100.00**

It can clearly be seen from the above table, the variation in the response pattern of the official of the two selected districts. In Bareilly district a considerable majority (66.67 per cent) of the respondents expressed 'to a large extent' that the decentralised planning model is an appropriate model for development. This also goes along the general line of thinking about the model. About one-third of the respondents favoured the response option of 'to some extent'. In Gorakhpur district the officials are equally divided (42.86 per cent) about the two response options. It can be argued on the basis of these responses that though the percentage varies the respondents have given positive signal to decentralised planning model for development.

As we have reported earlier that the Constitutional Amendment Act of 1992 made the composition of District Planning Committees obligatory. The decentralised planning model was to be made operative through the District Planning Committees. In view of this Constitutional provision every State across the country was obliged to constitute the District Planning Committee as per the provision of the Constitution. In Uttar Pradesh also steps had to be taken to constitute these DPCs. It has been alleged that there was delay in constituting the District Planning Committees for one reason or the other. We wanted to know from the officials about the timing of the constitution of these Committees in the State. Their response is being given in the Table 44 below.

Table 44. Constitution of the District Planning Committee

Year	*Percentage of Bareilly*	*Percentage of Gorakhpur*
2007	50.00	42.85
2008	50.00	57.15
No Idea	Nil	Nil
Total	**100.00**	**100.00**

It can be seen from the table above that the respondents in both the selected districts gave their options for the constitution of the DPC as 2007 and 2008. In Bareilly, the respondents were equally divided over the two options. In Gorakhpur however, majority of the respondents (57.15 per cent) opined that it was constituted in 2008 whereas the rest opted for 2007.

The formal constitution of the DPC did get delayed in the State for some reasons. The respondents in both the selected districts were unanimous on the point when expressed that there was delay in constituting the DPC in the State. We, therefore, wanted to know from the official respondents as to what they think would have been the main reason for delay in getting the DPC constituted. The responses received are given in the Table 45 below.

Table 45. Reasons for Delay in Constituting the DPC

Reason	*Percentage of Bareilly*	*Percentage of Gorakhpur*
Lack of Political Will	66.66	57.15
No Idea	33.34	42.85
Total	**100.00**	**100.00**

A glance at the table above would make it clear that majority of the respondents in both the selected districts opined that due to lack of political will the constitution of DPCs in the State got delayed. It is, however, interesting to note that a considerable percentage of respondent in both the selected districts said that they had no idea of the reason that delayed the formation of DPC in the State.

Once the District Planning Committees were constituted and started functioning, the logical question arises about their effective and proper working. In view of this we wanted to know from the respondents as to how far they think that the DPCs are performing their task satisfactorily. The responses received are given in the Table 46 below.

Table 46. Performance of DPCs in the State

Extent	*Percentage of Bareilly*	*Percentage of Gorakhpur*
To a large extent	16.67	28.57
To some extent	50.00	42.86
Not at all	33.33	28.57
Total	**100.00**	**100.00**

It can be clearly seen from the figures given above that responses in the two selected districts vary. In Bareilly district in the response category of 'to some extent' was opted by 50 per cent of the respondents. It is interesting to note that one-third respondents opted for 'not at all' response category. It therefore indicates that the officials are not satisfied with the performance of the DPC. In Gorakhpur district, the respondents are equally divided with 28.57 per cent response to two different response options. One group of respondent expressed 'to a large extent' response category and on the contrary the same percentage reported for 'not at all' response category. It provides a mixed response so far as the performance of the DPC in the district is concerned. About 43 per cent respondents however, in Gorakhpur opined that they are 'to some extent' satisfied with the performance of the DPC in the district. It can be observed here that since the DPC were constituted late the officials could not get enough time to access their performance.

After getting the opinion of the officials of the two selected districts about the performance of the DPCs we wanted to ascertain from the respondents about the formulation and consolidation of plan. Since planning is a time-bound activity, adherence to time schedule becomes important. We have already reported about the consolidation and preparation of plan in earlier pages. We here wanted to ascertain for the officials as to how far they think the DPC was able to formulate the plan in time. The responses so received are being presented in the Table 47 as under.

Table 47. DPC has been Able to Formulate the Plan in Time

Extent	*Percentage of Bareilly*	*Percentage of Gorakhpur*
To a large extent	16.67	14.29
To some extent	66.66	71.42
Not at all	16.67	14.29
Total	**100.00**	**100.00**

The information given in the table above provides by and large, similar response pattern with minor variations in percentages in response options. There appears to be a general opinion about the question of adhering to time schedule for plan formulation. A considerable majority of official respondents in both the selected districts gave 'to some extent' response option. In Bareilly district, 66.66 per cent of the respondents opted for this option. In Gorakhpur, the percentage response was slightly higher (71.42 per cent). It is interesting to note that a similar percentage of response, though small, opted for two contradictory response options. In Bareilly 16.67 per cent respondents opined for an option of 'to large extent' while a similar percentage opted for 'not at all'. In Gorakhpur also we find the similar response pattern with slightly reduced percentage. In over all analysis we can observe that since these percentages are small, therefore, not much inference can be drawn. But overwhelming majority opined, though to some extent only, that the plans were completed in time.

The plan preparation is a serious and complex exercise. The plan has to be a realistic one in order to serve the people in right earnest. The hypothetical plan would not serve much purpose. The district plans have to address the needs and requirements of the area and the people. We wanted to know from the official participants as well as other officials as to how far the district plans have been realistic. We wanted to know whether the members of the DPC made serious efforts to make the district plans realistic. The responses received are given in the Table 48 below.

Table 48. DPC Member Made Serious Efforts to Make a Realistic Plan

Extent	*Percentage of Bareilly*	*Percentage of Gorakhpur*
To a large extent	16.67	14.29
To some extent	66.66	71.42
Not at all	16.67	14.29
Total	**100.00**	**100.00**

It can clearly be seen that figures given in the table above provide almost similar indications. An overwhelming majority of the respondents in both the selected districts have expressed that the District Planning Committees have been able to put in their efforts in order to make a realistic district plan. In Bareilly district 66.66 per cent of the official respondents opined that 'to some extent' the DPC members made serious efforts to make the plan realistic whereas the percentage for Gorakhpur district is still higher (71.42 per cent) for the same category of response. Further, we observe that in Bareilly district very low percentage (16.67 per cent) officials opted for contradictory response option. They said that the DPC members 'to a large extent' made efforts to make a realistic district plan and on the contrary similar percentage (16.67 per cent) said 'not at all' as their response option.

One of the important functions of planning is to determine the priorities for various sectors apart from allocation of resources. The fixation of priorities in the decentralised planning process also assures significance as on the basis of these priorities their activity would follow. We, therefore, wanted to know the opinion of the official respondents as to whether priorities for the State and the district remains the same or they vary from district to district. The responses received from the official respondents are presented in the Table 49 as under.

Table 49. Priorities for the State and District Vary or Not

Extent	*Percentage of Bareilly*	*Percentage of Gorakhpur*
Uniform	16.67	57.14
Vary	83.33	42.86
Total	**100.00**	**100.00**

The figures given in the table above show a clear variation in the response pattern of the two districts. In Bareilly district, the majority of the respondents (83.33 per cent) have clearly opined that the plan priorities for the State and that of the district are not the same, they vary. A very thin percentage of respondents (16.67 per cent) opined that they are uniform for the State as well as for the district. However, the response pattern in Gorakhpur district seems to be different than that of Bareilly district. In Gorakhpur district slightly more than half (57.14 per cent) of the respondents expressed that the plan priorities for the State and that of the district are uniform. This opinion is in contrast to that of Bareilly district response. Further, less than half (42.86 per cent) of the respondents expressed that priorities for the State and the districts varies as they are not the same. This response pattern provides a confusing and contrasting shade of opinion and therefore no final view can be .taken on this question.

After putting the question on the nature of priorities for the State and district plan, we wanted to ascertain from the officials whether these priorities take into consideration the needs of the area. We find that the planning has to be based on the needs and requirements of the area in order to be effective and realistic. In view of this, a subsequent query was considered important to probe. The respondents were asked to give their opinion as to how far the priorities fixed by the DPC are as per the needs of the area. The responses given by the respondents are given in the Table 50 below.

Table. 50. Priorities Fixed by the DPC are as Per the Need of the Area

Extent	*Percentage of Bareilly*	*Percentage of Gorakhpur*
To a large extent	33.23	14.29
To some extent	50.00	71.42
Not at all	16.67	14.29
Total	**100.00**	**100.00**

It can be clearly seen from the figures given in above table that there are considerable variations in the response pattern of the two selected districts. In Bareilly, we notice that 50 per cent of the respondents expressed that priorities fixed by the DPC are 'to some extent' according to the needs of the area. About one-third respondents opined that the priorities fixed by the DPC are 'to a large extent' as per the need of the area. Only a very limited percentage (16.67 per cent) expressed that it is 'not at all' as per the need of the area. The figures for the district Gorakhpur present slightly different picture. A considerable percentage (71.42 per cent) of the respondents in the district opined that the priorities fixed by the DPC are 'to some extent' as per the need of the area. As against this opinion a small percentage of respondents seem to be divided on the two contradictory options. It is noteworthy that 14.29 per cent respondents favoured the option 'not at all' while the rest 14.29 per cent expressed that priorities fixed by the DPC are 'to a large extent' as per the need of the area. Under the circumstances, it become rather difficult to have a realistic opinion as to whether the priority fixed by the DPC were indeed according to the needs of the area.

We have discussed in the earlier chapter the strategies followed by the policy planners for growth and development of the country. A number of experiments in rural development sector can be seen during all these year of planned development. There has been a custom anxiety to know whether the strategies followed by India in earlier days are better or the one that are presently being followed by the planning bodies. In view of this, we asked the respondents as to how far they think the strategies followed in the earlier days were effective. Their responses are being presented in the Table 51 below.

Table 51. Effectiveness of the Planning Strategies

Extent	*Percentage of Bareilly*		*Percentage of Gorakhpur*	
	Earlier	*Present*	*Earlier*	*Present*
To a large extent	Nil	50.00	14.29	71.43
To some extent	33.33	50.00	71.42	28.57
Not at all	66.37	Nil	14.29	Nil
Total	**100.00**	**100.00**	**100.00**	**100.00**

The above table clearly shows that the responses given by the respondents in the two selected districts quite vary. In Bareilly district the officials opined in favour of the present strategies. It is interesting to note that 50 per cent of the respondents favoured the present strategies 'to a large extent' while the rest 50 per cent opted for the option of 'to some extent'. So far as the earlier strategies are concerned none of the respondents opined to the response category 'to a large extent'. A considerable majority (66.37 per cent) of the respondents expressed that the earlier strategies are 'not at all' effective whereas one-third of them opined for 'to some extent'. In Gorakhpur district the response pattern of the officials seems to be quite different than that of Bareilly district. For the earlier strategies in Gorakhpur a considerable majority (71.42 per cent) expressed that it is effective only 'to some extent'. A very limited and identical percentage (14.29 per cent) opted for two contradictory responses. One of the options said 'not at all' whereas the other option expressed 'to a large extent'. There appears to be a clear perception of the officials so far as the present strategies are concerned. A considerable majority (71.43 per cent) expressed that the present strategies are effective 'to a large extent' while the remaining 28.57 per cent opted for 'to some extent' option.

We have seen a number of changes being brought about in the decentralised planning process. In this scheme of things the District Planning Committees had been assigned a specific task of consolidation of the district plan. All these new changes in the overall scheme of things a change in perspective was also expected from the people who will actually be performing the task. In view of this we wanted to know from the participants as to how far they think that the new strategy of decentralised planning has attracted change in the perspective. The answers received are given in the Table 52 below.

Table 52. New Strategy has Effected Change in the Perspective

Extent	*Percentage of Bareilly*	*Percentage of Gorakhpur*
To a large extent	Nil	28.57
To some extent	83.33	57.14
Not at all	16.67	14.29
Total	**100.00**	**100.00**

The figures given in the above table clearly indicate the variation in the response pattern of the official of the two selected districts. In Bareilly an absolute majority of respondents

(83.33 per cent) expressed that the new strategy has effected the change in the perspective but only 'to some extent'. A very small percentage of respondents (16.67 per cent) opined that it 'not at all' effected change in the perspective. However, the respondents in the district of Gorakhpur provide a different response pattern. In the response category of 'to a large extent' only 28.57 per cent of the respondents expressed that new strategy effected change in the 'not at all' response category. A majority of the respondents (57.14 per cent) have expressed that the new strategy had effected change in perspective but 'to some extent'. A very nominal percentage of 14.29 per cent opined in favour of 'not al all' response category.

Institutional Set up and Networking

Any organisational activity would require a proper institutional set up and where there are a number of agencies involved then a proper networking becomes important for successful planning activity. In view of the importance of institutional set up and networking we wanted to know from the official respondents as to how far they agree that there are a large number of institutions dealing with decentralise planning. Their responses are being given in the Table 53 below.

Table. 53. Multiplicity of Agencies in Decentralised Planning

Extent	*Percentage of Bareilly*	*Percentage of Gorakhpur*
To a large extent	66.6	28.47
To some extent	16.67	57.14
Not at all	16.67	14.29
Total	**100.00**	**100.00**

The figures given in the table above clearly indicate the wide variation in the response pattern of the two selected districts in the State. In Bareilly district the official respondents (66.66 per cent) expressed that 'to a large extent' there are multiple agencies involved in the decentralised planning. In the remaining percentage response equal percentage of responses were opted for two contradictory responses. The first option of 'to some extent' was given by 16.67 per cent while the remaining 16.67 per cent expressed to 'not at all' response option. The situation in Gorakhpur district is rather different than we noticed for the other district. In Gorakhpur 57.14 per cent official respondents expressed that 'to some extent' there is multiplicity of agencies in decision-making.

About 28.57 per cent respondents opined 'to a large extent' response option. A thin percentage of 14.29 per cent respondents felt that multiples agencies 'not at all' exist in decentralised planning process.

It is general impression that multiplicity of agencies does affect the decentralised planning process. It makes the process more complex and cumbersome. It is also felt that multiplicity of agencies is in the nature of the planning process as different organisations are involved in the process. We wanted to know from the official respondents as to how far they think that multiplicity of institutions affects the decentralised planning process. The responses received are being presented in the Table 54 below.

Table 54. Multiplicity of Institutions Affects Decentralised Planning

Extent	*Percentage of Bareilly*	*Percentage of Gorakhpur*
To a large extent	50.00	29.57
To some extent	33.33	57.14
Not at all	16.67	14.29
Total	**100.00**	**100.00**

The figures given in the above table show a varying response pattern. The percentages given provide two different responses in the two selected districts. In Bareilly, 50 per cent of the respondents expressed 'to a large extent' that multiplicity of institutions affects the decentralised planning. As against this about one-third respondents argued that it affects only 'to some extent'. A very small percentage (16.67 per cent) of the respondents opted for 'not at all' response option. In Gorakhpur district, the official respondents provide a different response pattern. About 29 per cent respondents have expressed that 'to a large extent' multiplicity of institution affects the decentralised planning. About 57 per cent of the respondents opted for 'to some extent' response option and only 14.29 per cent opted for 'not at all' response option.

In the earlier pages of the report, we have noted various issues related with Panchayati Raj institutions. We have already impressed upon the importance of Panchayati Raj institutions for decentralised planning. The Panchayati Raj institutions in fact are involved in the whole process of decentralised planning. In view of the importance of Panchayati Raj institutions for decentralised planning we wanted to know from the official respondents as to how far they think that Panchayati Raj institutions have helped the cause of decentralised planning. The responses are being given in the Table 55 below.

Table 55. Panchayati Raj Institutions Helped the Cause of Decentralised Planning

Extent	*Percentage of Bareilly*	*Percentage of Gorakhpur*
To a large extent	66.67	14.29
To some extent	33.33	71.42
Not at all	Nil	14.29
Total	**100.00**	**100.00**

It can be clearly seen from the figures given in the table above that the opinions of respondents generally vary in the two selected districts. In Bareilly, we notice that 66.67 per cent respondents agreed 'to a large extent' that Panchayati Raj institutions helped the cause of decentralised planning. It can be seen as a dominant expression of the respondents. In addition 33.33 per cent respondents expressed their opinion in 'to some extent' response category. In Gorakhpur, we find different shades of opinion. A considerable majority 71.42 per cent of the respondents opted for 'to some extent' response option which shows that the respondents agreed that Panchayati Raj institutions helped the cause of decentralised planning 'to some extent.

We have already noted that there are various institutions involved in the decentralised planning process. In such a process where more than one institutions are involved. Co-ordination occupies an important place in overall scheme of things as lack of co-ordination can create problems in the planning process which would affect the achievement of results. In view of the importance of co-ordination, we wanted to know from the official respondents as to how far they feel satisfied with co-ordination amongst the various agencies involved in the decentralised planning process. Their answers are given in the Table 56 below.

Table 56. Satisfaction with Co-ordination amongst Various Institutions

Extent	*Percentage of Bareilly*	*Percentage of Gorakhpur*
To a large extent	33.33	14.28
To some extent	50.00	42.86
Not at all	16.67	42.86
Total	**100.00**	**100.00**

The figures presented in the table above clearly indicate the variation in the response pattern of the two selected districts. In Bareilly about one-third (33.3 per cent) respondents expressed satisfaction with the issue of co-ordination amongst the various institutions 'to a large extent'. It is noteworthy that half of the respondents expressed satisfaction 'to some extent' only. A narrow percentage (16.67 per cent) of the respondents opted for 'not at all' response option. In the district Gorakhpur an identical percentage of 42.86 of the official respondent expressed contradictory opinion. It may be noted that one group of respondents opined 'to some extent' while the other opted for 'not at all' response option. Only a nominal percentage (16.28 per cent) expressed that they are satisfied 'to a large extent'.

We have already noted that there are various organisations and agencies involved in the decentralised planning process. In view of the important role of the decentralised planning in plan formulation and consolidation it is quite pertinent that the institutions involve should take their role seriously to get the desired results. We therefore, wanted the opinion of the official on this issue. The respondents were thus, asked to give their opinion on how far they think that the institutions involved have taken their jobs seriously. Their opinion is being presented in the Table as under.

Table 57. Institutions Involved have Taken their Job Seriously

Extent	*Percentage of Bareilly*	*Percentage of Gorakhpur*
To a large extent	16.67	Nil
To some extent	66.66	85.71
Not at all	16.67	14.29
Total	**100.00**	**100.00**

The opinion expressed by the respondents of the two selected districts vary can be seen from the figures given in the table above. In Bareilly a considerable majority (66.66 per cent) of the respondents expressed 'to some extent' for the job being taken seriously by the people. An identical percentage 16.67 of the respondents expressed contradictory option. One group of respondents opined for the response options 'to a large extent' while the other gave 'not at all' response option. The response pattern for Gorakhpur varies than that of Bareilly. In Gorakhpur none of the respondents opted for 'to a large extent' option. A very large majority of respondents (85.71

per cent) have opted for 'to some extent' response option. Only a small percentage (14.29 per cent) opted for 'not at all' response option.

We are all aware that planning requires special ability and skill. It is not the laymen's domain. The people who are involved in the decentralised planning process should generally have the required skill to discharge their responsibilities effectively. We thus, wanted to know from the officials the actual situation of the field. We, therefore, asked them as to how far they think that the institutions engaged in the planning process have the required skills. Their answers are being given in the Table 58 below.

Table 58. Institutions have the Required Skills for Planning

Extent	*Percentage of Bareilly*	*Percentage of Gorakhpur*
To a large extent	16.67	14.29
To some extent	83.33	71.42
Not at all	Nil	14.29
Total	**100.00**	**100.00**

The figures given in the table above provide opinion in the same response category with variation in percentage. In Bareilly 83.33 per cent of the respondents opted for 'to some extent' category response while in Gorakhpur this response percentage is 71.42 for the same category. This only indicates that official in both the districts opted for this response. In response category of 'to a large extent' also there is marginal difference in response percentage. In the overall analysis we can say that the officials have opined that the institutions engaged in the planning process have the required skill for the job in hand.

We have presented a detailed analysis of various issues connected with decentralised planning based on the primary data collected through the questionnaires. We have also discussed the formation of District Planning Committees in various States including the selected States of Uttar Pradesh and Andhra Pradesh the non-official and the official respondents have by and large, agreed with the important role of the DPCs in the decentralised planning process. They have opined that the new strategy should be able to address the issue connected with planning and development.

5

Problem Areas in Decentralised Planning

Decentralised planning has been the core concern in the planning effort from the very beginning of planned development approach in the country. But special attention and focus were given to it after the 73rd and 74th Constitutional Amendments. As a result of this, we notice several changes in the planning structure at the district level wherein it was made imperative to constitute District Planning Committees. As a matter of fact, the State Governments across the country took steps to formally launch the decentralised planning process as per the Constitutional positions. In pursuance of these Amendments the District Planning Committees were constituted to give shape to decentralised planning by the States.

It is now quite some time since these DPCs were formally constituted and have started functioning. During this short span of their existence a number of problems have been encountered in the functioning of the District Planning Committees. The present chapter proposes to briefly examine these problems which affect the effective functioning of the DPCs and which need attention for proper decentralised planning process. Since there are quite a few areas where the problems have been reported, we would try to take them one after the other.

Participation Related Problems

Decentralised planning, by its very nature, has to participative. It was initially anticipated that it will encourage local participation in the planning process at the district level. The participation is ensured through the District Planning Committees where the members take part in formulation and consolidation of the District Plan. The composition of the DPC is such where the local Members of Parliament (MPs.) and Member of the Legislative Assembly (MLAs) have also been included as member of the DPCs. It has created its own problem. It has been reported that their mere presence in the meetings of the District Planning Committees often inhibits the discussion and in a way restricts the participation of other local members. The MPs and the MLAs having strong political base influence the deliberations and the decisions with their narrow partisan interest which other local members generally do not appreciate, but desist from protesting due to their weak political base and support. This was highlighted by a number of non-official respondents who were members of the DPC.

It is worth recollecting that initially it was thought that local MPs and MLAs should be taken into consideration while preparing and consolidating the district plan. Since there is special fund allocated to Members of Parliament for the purpose of taking up development works in their respective constituency. This could be taken into account while consolidating the plan for the district. But the real situation in the field is reported to be different. The projects taken up with the funds for the MP's quota generally do not form an integral part of the district plan. It is therefore, argued that the purpose of associating the MPs and MLAs with the district planning process served the purpose only partially. It is being felt that it has created communication gap amongst the members of the DPC which in terms affects the planning process. It is also being mentioned that since a considerable number of MPs and MLAs belong to the other side of the law this further increases the gap amongst various members of the DPC. It is therefore, a problem that affects general participation of the members in planning process.

The participation of the members is hampered by other considerations as well. During the course of our field study several non-official members argued that attending the meetings of the DPCs require time which the member give at their own cost. They argued that at times members are not able to attend the meetings because of their own personal pre-occupation. Consequently, local participation suffers. In order to encourage members to attend the meetings of the DPC, several non-official respondents argued for giving honorarium to members. This would serve as a motivating factor for the members to attend the meetings of the DPC.

Ego Problems

During the course of our field study problem related with personal ego's have been reported. The decentralised planning process involves people of various shades including MPs and MLAs apart from other elected and nominated members in the District Planning Committee. We have already pointed out earlier in the report about the role and importance of MPs and MLAs and the reaction of other local members of the DPC. A clash of egos have been reported which the respondents pointed out. It had been observed that once the MPs and MLAs come to the meetings of the DPCs, they receive all the attention from the officials who are present therein whereas other member's presence is hardly given any importance. The members of the DPC get no proper respect and attention from the officials. The MPs and MLAs try to push through their personal and political agenda in the presence of other local members who generally get little attention which hurts their egos. We are aware that the MPs have their own development fund which is supposed to be utilised in their constituency. At the same, we have observed that the projects under the MPs fund generally are not part of the District Plan. But the MPs and MLAs do influence the decision in the District Planning Committees where the District plan is being formulated and consolidated. The problem could be minimised if the MPs and MLAs take the local members into confidence while pushing their political agenda for the district. This may help improve communication level and to some extent sort out the ego problem of local members.

On the contrary the opinion expressed by the officials does not support the complaint raised by the members resulting in ego clashes. It was pointed that the local members are not quite aware of the planning process. They have little knowledge as to how the plans have to be formulated and consolidated. Many of them are confused about the decentralised planning process. The officials expressed that there should be qualified people and experts in place of political nominated members. It can be inferred that although the members are ill-equipped for the decentralised planning process, they need attention and respect from the officials as well as others which they find lacking and this creates problem and results in ego clashes.

Plan Preparation

Problems have been reported in the preparation and consolidation of district plan. Initially, it was conceived that a village plan has to be prepared. The government had already prescribed the method and the process of preparing a village plan. Once the village plans have been prepared, they would be sent to the Block office. At the block level, it was expected that a Block Plan would be prepared taking the village plan as the base. The Block plan was supposed to be a consolidation of village plan. Once the Block plans are completed they would be sent to the district. At the district level, it was anticipated that the District Plan would consolidate the Block Plan and prepare a plan for the district. Thus, a District Plan includes plans for the development of the village and the blocks which have been prepared as has been initially conceived. This was supposed to be the decentralised planning process wherein the plans are being prepared on the basis of local needs and aspirations by the representative of the local people.

During the course of our field study problems have been reported in the planning process. Members apprised that often the MPs and MLAs want their own proposals included in the district plan instead of the plan which have come through the blocks. Members of Parliament have the privilege of having their own constituency development fund which has to be utilised in the constituency through various development schemes under the fund. Members often insist upon the inclusion of their schemes generally at the district level in the district plan. The problem arises because such schemes are not part of the plans which is coming from the village panchayats through the Kshetra Panchayat. Since these schemes are out of the regular plan process, the local members dispute their inclusion in the district plan document as such as we have already noted that the decentralised planning process is an integrated planning process which are based on the participation of the people in that process. It is therefore, argued that if these schemes are intended to be included in the plan document, the proper process should be followed so that it does not create any misunderstanding amongst the various members of the D.P.C. Unless such a procedure is adhered to, the problem will continue to be there.

Lack of Co-ordination

One of the problems reported by the non-official members was related with co-ordination. Planning involves various people and agencies for an effective and efficient planning exercise, co-ordination amongst various agencies as well as others, involved becomes a sine-qua-non. During the course of our study several non-official members observed that there is a lack of co-ordination amongst the members of the DPC. There is no coordinated effort on the part of the members to help the planning process achieve the desired objectives. Lack of co-ordination is visible at different levels of decentralised planning process. It is not confined to any one level of planning exercise we observed this at all the three levels of decentralised planning process.

It has been experienced during the course of field study that a number of agencies are involved in consolidating and formulating the plans at different levels. We have already reported about the various agencies involved along with the opinion of the officials and non-officials in the earlier chapter. It was pointed by the people associated with planning that there is a lack of co-ordination amongst various agencies involved in the decentralised planning process. This lack of co-ordination amongst the agencies involved led to affect adversely the decentralised planning process. Many a times because of this lack of co-ordination there is delay in the process of consolidation of the plan document. It is interesting to note that lack of co-ordination is not confined to any one level of the planning process. It can be seen at different levels of the planning process. The delay in the plan formulation and consolidation often results in a blame game. It was observed during the field study that in order to explain the delay in the process, one agency blames the other for the delay and the process goes on. The lack of co-ordination is definitely seems to be a problem that needs attention of various members as well as the officials connected with decentralised planning process to make it efficient and effective.

Lack of Transparency

Of late there has been considerable focus on the transparency aspects in the governing process. It is argued that lack of transparency breeds inefficiency and corruption in administration. In the case of decentralised planning with reference to District Planning Committees the non-official members complained lack of transparency in the planning process. They argued that transparency should be there in various issues connected with public affairs while discussing the plan allocation, plan priorities, financial matter and the like. Since there is lack of transparency, various members complain about lack of information to be provided to them regarding plan formulation in the district. We have already noted that decentralised planning is a participative process. The members therefore, should get adequate information about the various issues connected with the plan formulation and consolidation of the plan at the district level.

The lack of transparency gets reflected where the funds are being allocated in the plan. There are political pulls and pressure and influential members influence the process in their own interest. There is hardly any clear cut demarcation of funds for different levels of panchayats and municipalities. Members have, therefore, argued that there should be clear cut demarcation of funds for different levels of panchayats and municipalities. Once there is a clear cut demarcation, there would be little scope for manipulation. Members then can raise their voices in case of deviation. This will maintain transparency in the process for plan allocation and other activities related with planning process.

Lack of Training Skill

This is a common perception that plan formulation is a technical job which requires skill. In the decentralised planning process too requirements remain the same. The plan formulation at the level of village, block and district would require manpower which is knowledgeable, trained and skillful. During the course of the field study the officials did raise the problem of lack of training for the members responsible for plan formulation and plan consolidation at different levels of decentralised planning process. It was alleged that the members had little knowledge and training for plan formulation. Since these members are elected ones for them there is no requirement of training in the field of plan preparation. In the absence of proper training the members fail to understand the planning process. Most of the members use this forum for lodging their personal complaint. The officials therefore, argued for a proper training of the members for plan formulation. The members should be educated so that they can understand the planning process. For the present lack of training and skill in the field of plan preparation is being considered a genuine problem that hamper proper planning? In this context, it has also been pointed out that the training should include software as well to facilitate efficient and effective planning exercise. The officials have also argued that there should be qualified experts who should serve as members instead of elected members, who will solve the problem of lack of training and skill for the purpose of planning.

The need for training for plan formulation has been felt by several other agencies, governmental as well as non-governmental which have addressed the issue earlier. In view of this, perhaps a provision for taking assistance from the experts in plan formulation does exist. However, it leaves much to be desired so far as the proper plan formulation exercises at the district and below is concerned. It is because of this that the lack of training is felt as a problem in decentralised planning process. Here, it can also be mentioned that the officials pointed out during the field study that the members are not well aware of their duties and responsibilities. It, therefore, further supplements the need for a proper training schedule for the members so that they get well aware of their duties and responsibilities along with acquiring some knowledge and skill about the decentralised planning process and plan formulation exercise.

Problems of General Nature

Apart from the problems discussed in the earlier pages, there are some other problems which have been felt during the course of the study. We have already noted problems in connection with participation by members in the meetings of the District Planning Committee. Members expressed concern over the delay in calling the meetings. It has been reported by the non-official members that the meetings are generally not held as per the prescribed schedule. They have, therefore, argued that the meetings should generally be held as per the prescribed schedule. Since these meetings are not held as frequently as required the necessary debate and discussions could not be held. Members also do not get adequate time to prepare and discuss and present their view point in such meetings. They feel deprived of an opportunity of effective participation in these meetings which is the main forum for presenting one's view point. Many of them argued that the meetings should be held with three months duration which would mean that every quarterly these meetings should be held.

Another problem which has been referred by the officials is connected with the proposals submitted by the members. Most of the people submitted by the members are not within the proper frame. It becomes difficult at the time of consolidation of the district plan to take all those proposals within the plan format for various reasons. The officials were therefore, of the view that there should be specific criteria for acceptance of the proposals submitted by the representatives. This would facilitate the consolidation process and reduce problems arising out of such vague plan proposals.

The official members pointed out that there is no proper method of monitoring and evaluation of the performance of plans. It has been alleged that once the plan gets finalised and implemented there is hardly any mechanism for monitoring and evaluation of the plan projects. In the absence of this there is little awareness about the actual results obtained from the planned effort. The officials, therefore, argued for a proper monitoring and evaluation of the plans. They have favoured a sub-committee at the district level to perform the task of monitoring and evaluation.

The non-official members reported about the lack of infrastructure facility at various levels of decentralised planning set up. Members complained about the lack of proper seating arrangements during the meeting of District Planning Committee. Since the members faced problems in this regard they suggested that there should be some arrangements for sitting only for the DPC members. This would ease the problem to some extent.

These are in brief some of the problems encountered by the members in the decentralised planning process which is made operative through the District Planning Committees.

6

Conclusions and Suggestions

The post-independent India experimented with quite a few developmental models for its growth and development. Amongst these tested models the decentralised planning model got priority of attention from the policy planners for various reasons. The Community Development Programmes launched in the early fifties were an experiment in participative planning a core concern in decentralised planning process. Balwantrai Mehta Committee recommended for a three-tier structure of Panchayati Raj that adds another dimension to decentralised planning. Subsequently, we find the Fourth Plan document provides for the Growth Centers, and the issuing of guidelines for the district planning by the Planning Commission in 1965 makes a strong case for decentralised planning in the country. The concern shown and the efforts taken by the Government of India shows that despite the failure of district planning or regional planning to take off in India, the need for decentralised planning has continuously been felt. We can very well see these efforts through the successive Five Year Plan which have been formulated and implemented through all these decades. At the same time, it is generally alleged that decentralised planning could not be successfully implemented across the States in the country and there are several reasons to explain this state of affairs.

The decade of nineties provides new lease of life to local governance and decentralised planning too finds priority in that scheme of things. The 73rd and 74th Constitutional Amendment

Acts of 1992 gave a new definition to local governance by giving local governing institutions—both urban and rural - a constitutional status which was considered a historic achievement by many in the constitutional history of India. The decentralised planning process too got a shot in the arm as the Article 243ZD provides for the constitution of District Planning Committees for the purpose of preparing plans for the district. In pursuance of this constitutional provision, States took steps to constitute District Planning Committees in their respective States. Some States constituted the DPC in time, whereas in some other States it got delayed on various grounds.

In this context, a reference may be made of the Second Round Table Conference which made several recommendations about decentralised planning. Some of these recommendations were considered by the Approach Paper of the Eleventh Five Year Plan. These are as under:

- District Planning Committees ought to be constituted in every State by the end of the financial year 2004-2005 in accordance with the procedure laid down in Article 243ZD (2).
- All States ought to make provision by law, utilising the functions and procedure of DPCs.
- District Planning Committees ought to take into account the area's resources endowment, people, felt needs, and their relative absorption capacity.
- Each level of Panchayats and Municipalities ought to prepare perspective Five Year Plan and Annual Plan as provided in the Constitution which could be considered by the DPC.
- The State must specify institution, organisation and individuals to assist panchayats, municipalities and DPCs in preparing plans in accordance with Article 243ZD(3)(b).
- The State must indicate extent and type of available resources to each Panchayat level and Municipalities as per Article 243ZD in order to facilitate planning.
- Central Government could consider establishing a mechanism to pool all Central Government and Finance Commission's resources, for channeling them to Panchayats.
- States must strengthen the training of PRIs so that planning at the district and sub-district levels is based on as indication of the available resources.

In view of these recommendations, the Planning Commission wrote to the State Governments to consider several points raised here. In pursuance of these State took steps to constitute the DPCs. It, however, remained a matter of anxiety as to the effectiveness or otherwise of the DPCs is concerned. It called for an objective assessment to understand the ground level situation before making any observation and having a concluding view points.

In view of the above, the present study was proposed to be undertaken. The study was proposed with the following main objectives:

- To study the organisation and structure of decentralised planning with focus on District Planning Committees.
- To examine the methods and procedures of decentralised planning with particular reference to District Planning Committees.
- To assess the effectiveness of decentralised planning in achieving goals and targets set forth for development.
- To identify the difference in development perspective in the selected areas with and without District Planning Committee.
- To study specifically the role of District Planning Committee in decentralised planning.
- To identify the problem areas in decentralised planning.
- To suggest changes in the present organisation and process of decentralised planning, in case needed, for better development administration.

Scope and Methodology

Broadly speaking, the study had India in perspective. Since decentralised planning is under the State List of Subjects under the Constitution, variations of various nature were bound to be there. In order to have a detailed analysis of the organisation and process of decentralised planning, two States namely, Andhra Pradesh from the south and Uttar Pradesh from north were initially selected. The detailed primary as well as secondary sources of data have specifically been collected from these States.

Further, two districts from each of the selected States were selected for collection of detailed information from the field. The selected districts were as under:

1. Andhra Pradesh
    1. Rangareddy
    2. Chittoor

2. Uttar Pradesh
    1. Gorakhpur
    2. Bareilly

The data has thus, been collected from these two States and the selected districts therein – The study has made use of both the sources of data, i.e., the primary as well as secondary. The primary sources of data were collected through two different sets questionnaire – one for the officials and the other for the non-officials, connected with the decentralised planning process. The secondary sources include information collected through books, journals, newspaper reports and other published materials.

Profile of the Universe

For the purposes of detailed collection of information two States as state earlier were selected namely, Andhra Pradesh and Uttar Pradesh. A brief profile of the selected States is being given here.

A. Andhra Pradesh

It is the fifth largest State in India and forms the major link between the north and the south of India. It is the biggest and most populous State in southern part of India. It is bounded by Madhya Pradesh, Chhatisgarh and Orissa in the north, the Bay of Bengal in the east, Tamil Nadu and Karnataka in the south and Maharashtra in the west.

As per the 2001 census, Andhra Pradesh had a total population of 75,727,541 of which 38,286,811 were males and the rest 37,440,730 were females. The sex ratio (females per thousand males) stood at 979. Andhra Pradesh is thus, the fifth largest State in India both in terms of area and population.

So far as the climate of the State is concerned, it receives rainfall from the South-West monsoon as well as the North-East monsoon. The first rainfall begins in the second week of June and it lasts till September while the second occur in October-November. The State's coastal area receives heavy rains during the North-East monsoon and is also subject to cyclone's conditions which cause enormous damage to residential accommodation and to standing crops. The State has a really hot summer but after the rain begins, there is a decline in the heat.

The State is dotted with hill ranges from the north to the south, running erratically down the middle of the country dividing it into western and eastern or coastal Andhra.

The State has two great rivers, Godavari and Krishna which spring from the western ghat in Maharashtra and flow eastward and joining the Bay of Bengal. Besides these two big rivers, there are the Tungabhadra, the Pennar and many other small rivers and rivulets.

The Caste Structure

Among the dwijas (twice-born castes) the Brahmans constitute about two-three per cent of the State's population. They are still in the large numbers in the bureaucracy, mass media, academic institutions and other vital professions such as law, scientific research, medicines and management.

The Vysas, known as Komatis in the State constitute another two-three per cent and are engaged in traditional occupation of trade, Rajus who claim to be Kshatriyas status are mostly confined to the north and central coastal region and may constitute about one per cent.

The non-Brahmin caste groups such as the Reddis, Kammas, Kapus and Velamas, whose main occupation has been cultivation, are the most important social groups in the State in terms of numerical strength, land control and access to political power.

Andhra Pradesh is one of the major States with a large concentration of the Scheduled Castes and Scheduled Tribes with about eight per cent of the total SC population of the country. There are about 33 tribes forming about seven per cent of the population of the State.

Various caste groups, which are known by the names of the traditional hereditary occupations, mainly artisan and service occupations, constitute a large portion of the population in Andhra Pradesh known as 'backward castes'.

This in brief is the profile of the State.

B. Uttar Pradesh

Uttar Pradesh is truly the heart of India situated in northern India and shares its border with Himachal, Punjab, Delhi, Madhya Pradesh, Bihar and International border with Nepal. It has an area of 2.94 million sq. km. Area-wise it is the fourth largest State in the country. It can be divided into three distinct *hypsographical* regions:

- The Himalayan region in the north
- The Gangetic plain in the center
- The Vindhya hills and plateau in the south.

The climate of the State is tropical monsoon, but variations exist because of difference in altitudes. The Himalayan region is cold. The average temperature varies in the plain from 3-40°C in January to 43-45°C in May and June. There are three distinct seasons from October to February, summer from March to mid-June and the rainy season from March to September.

The major rivers are the Ganga, Yamuna, Gomti, Ghaghra, Rapti, Sharyu and Ramganga.

The total population of the State as per Census of 2001 is 166,052,859 out of which 87,466,301 are males and the rest 78,856,558 are females. The sex ratio (females per thousand males) is 898.

The People

The central fact of the social order in Uttar Pradesh is the existence of the caste system among the Hindus who constitute the vast majority of the population. The broad hierarchies in the Hindu social system were the Brahmin, Kshatriya, Vaishya, Shudras and Achhuts or the untouchable. Further division-based on occupation gave rise to caste like Nai (Barbar), Dhobi (Washerman), Lohar (Blacksmith), Darji (Tailor) and all of them form a vital part of the village economy and life.

The greatest gift of Uttar Pradesh to human civilisation is the two epics, 'Ramayana' and 'Mahabharat' of the epic age. The territory of the State is watered by several streams culture, the two most significant being those generated by the teachings of Buddha and Mahavira, the 24th Jain Tirthankar.

The Districts

A-1—Rangareddy

The district selected for the study has a population of 3,755,064 out of which 1,839,227 are males and 1,735,837 are females. Amongst the total population Hindus constitute 86.62 per cent while Muslim constitutes only 11.41 per cent. The percentage of other religious groups is negligible. The Scheduled Castes constitute the 14.55 per cent of the total population.

For the administrative purposes the district is divided into sub-district, mainly they constitute rural and some have urban characteristics.

A-2—Chittoor

As per 2001 Census, the district had a total population of 3,745,275 out of which 1,889,690 are males and the rest 1,85,185 are females. Out of the total population, Hindus constitute 89.91per cent whereas Muslims constitute 9.15 per cent. The rest of religious groups had a very marginal percentage in the district.

For administrative purposes the district is divided into a number of sub-districts, mainly they constitute the rural but some are of urban nature.

B-1 —Bareilly

According to 2001 census, the district had a total population of 3,618,589 out of which 1,934.119 are males and the rest 1,684,470 are females, the Scheduled Castes constitute 12.65 per cent of the total population of the district. For administrative purposes the district is sub-divided into Sub-districts. There are six sub-districts in the district.

B-2—Gorakhpur

According to 2001 census, the district had a total population of 3,769,456 out of which 1,923,197 are males and the rest 1,846,259 are females. The religion-wise distribution shows that about 90 per cent of the population is Hindu while only nine per cent population is that of Muslim. The other religious groups constitute a very thin percentage. The Scheduled Caste population in the district constitutes about 22 per cent of the total population.

For administrative purposes the district is sub-divided into sub-districts. There are seven sub-districts in the district.

The District Planning Committees

The Composition and Working

The exercise of planning from below and that of participative planning started quite early in our planning process. However, the approach of the decentralised planning through the District Planning Committee came much later after considerable discussion and debate amongst policy planners. The present composition of the District Planning Committee owes to the provisions made in the Constitution of India. Article 243ZD of the Constitution provides that there shall be constituted in every State at the district level a District Planning Committee to consolidate the plan prepared by the Panchayats and the Municipalities in the district and to prepare a draft development plan for the district as a whole. The Constitution further provides that the Legislature of a State may, by-law, make provision with respect to:

(a) The composition of the District Planning Committees;

(b) The manner in which the seats in such Committees shall be filled;

provided that not less than four-fifth of the total number of members of such Committees shall be elected by, and from amongst the elected members of the Panchayat at the district level and of the Municipalities in the district in proportion to the ratio between the population of the rural areas and of the urban areas in the district;

(c) The functions relating to district planning which may be assigned to such Committees;

(d) The manner in which the Chairperson of such Committees shall be chosen.

The Constitution further indicates (Article 243-ZD(3) that every District Planning Committee shall, in preparing the draft development plan:

(a) Have regard to :

(i) Matters of common interest between the Panchayats and the Municipalities including spatial planning, sharing of matter and other physical and natural resources, the integrated development of infrastructure and environmental conservation;

(ii) The extent and type of available resources whether financial or otherwise;

(b) Consult such institutions and organisations as the Governor may, by order, specify.

Consequent upon the provision in the Constitution, the States took steps to constitute the District Planning Committees. It may be reported that the States took their own time to constitute these DPCs in their respective States. Some States like Uttar Pradesh took longer time than was needed in formally constituting the DPCs. This fact was corroborated during the field study wherein the respondents expressed that there was delay in constituting the DPCs in the State and a considerable percentage of respondents opined that owing to political consideration the delay was caused in constituting the DPC.

The information collected from most of the States show that elections have been held for the forming of District Planning Committees. However, whether or not they were actually held is another question altogether. Allegedly, the elections have been supervised by the district administration or State government—such elections are highly suspected. It has also been observed that there is no uniformity so far as the agencies supervising the elections to the District Planning Committees. It was argued that the State Election Commission would be the most desirable agency for conducting the elections to DPC, as they are expected to be more impartial than other agencies of the State government.

The issue linked with the Chairperson of the District Planning Committee has also been debated. We have noted three different patterns so far as the Chairperson of the DPCs is concerned:

- In some States the Chairperson/President CEO of the Zila Parishad or District Panchayat is the Chairperson of the DPC as well (Kerala, Andhra Pradesh, Rajasthan, Tamil Nadu and West Bengal),
- In some States the Minister-in-Charge of the district or any other State Minister is the Chairperson of the DPC (Orissa, Gujarat, Madhya Pradesh, and Maharashtra). In Himachal Pradesh, the Cabinet Minister of the State Government has been nominated as member and Chairperson of the DPCs.
- In Haryana, the Deputy Commissioner (DC) of the district is the Chairperson of the DPC.

Thus, we find no uniformity so far as the Chairperson of the DPC is concerned.

The main task assigned to the District Planning Committees is related with the preparation and consolidation of district plan. During the course of the study information about the consolidation of the district plan was collected from various States. The information so collected shows that while the sequence of the steps to be followed in consolidating rural and urban plans is similar, though the ground reality is entirely different. It has been reported that except Kerala, the functioning of the DPCs in other States is not at all effective. DPCs have not been able to effectively enable rural-urban linkages. Considerable planning is not taking place. Rural and urban local bodies are not working together on a common platform during the planning process to identify common projects/ resources requirements. Block-level integration of rural and urban plan is not carried out — the DPC guidelines recommended direct transmission of ULB plan to DPC. Inter-sector co-ordination was also felt to be a problem since it was realised on account of being against the status quo, old procedures are being followed for the sake of conveniences as well. The working of the DPCs suggests that several concrete steps need to be taken to further strengthen and decentralised the institutions of DPCs. Moreover, the DPCs need to be given adequate financial support as well as staff strength in order to enable them to perform their tasks effectively.

Role of District Planning Committees in Decentralised Planning

The decentralised planning was provided with a new status and a new approach after the local government reforms were put in place. As noted earlier, Article 243ZD provided for the formation of District Planning Committees and defined the purpose and the role of the Committees. Henceforth, the decentralised planning is being operative through the District Planning Committees across the country. We collected primary data through two sets of questionnaires (Annexure-I) from the officials as well as non-officials connected with decentralised planning process through the DPCs. We present in the following paragraphs very briefly analysis of that data particularly with reference to the selected State and the district.

There appears to be not much awareness and knowledge about the exact role and the functions assigned to the District Planning Committees in the decentralised planning process. A considerable percentage of the non-official members could not correctly recalled as to when the decentralised planning process began in their respective districts. They vaguely responded to the query about this. They were however, convincingly expressed that there was delay in constituting the DPCs in the State. A majority of the non-official respondents opined that decentralised planning strategy for development is effective and they felt largely satisfied with the decentralised planning strategy.

The District Planning Committees have been assigned specific role in preparing and consolidating the district plan. Information on this aspect was collected from the non-official respondents. The data shows that there is general dissatisfaction over the performance of the DPCs and where the satisfaction is reported, it is rather low. Sometimes it is the lack of motivation and some other time it may be the ego factor of the members that can be seen as a cause for the low-level of satisfaction. These were the issues which were identified during the course of the study.

In the preparation and consolidation of the district plan, the District Planning Committees are supposed to determine the priorities of the plan keeping in view the needs of the area and the people. This would determine the performance of the DPC. In this respect the members could not clearly indicate their options. To the query that whether the priorities for the State and the district are uniform or they vary, the opinion of the members suggest that they expressed in favour of uniform. This indicates that the priority for the State and that of the district remains the same which does not seem to be a realistic option. The DPC ought to figure out the priorities for the district as the needs of the area and the resources available. It goes to indicate that performance of the DPCs still needs a lot to be desired.

There has been a general observation of the members and the officials that planning requires knowledge and skill. The information collected and the data generated through the primary sources indicate that there has been lack of knowledge and skill amongst those responsible for plan preparation and consolidation. The elected members of the DPC are such where they hardly require this knowledge for their election purposes and it is not in their priority. Even others connected with the planning process do not possess adequate knowledge and skill that is required for proper and effective planning activity. This, therefore, gets reflected in the way the plans are prepared and also consolidated.

It has been observed that there are multiple agencies involved in the decentralised planning process. The multiplicity of agencies affected the decentralised planning process. This has been the opinion of both the category of respondents who were addressed for the purpose. Apart from the Panchayati Raj institutions and Municipalities, there are host of government departments as well agencies in the decentralised planning process at the district. The DPC in this plays an important role so far as the involvement of various agencies for planning is considered. The planning at this level would require the members of the DPC as well as the agencies to have common objectives rather than push partisan agenda. It would help counter the effects of the multiplicity of the agencies at the district level for planning.

Problem Areas in Decentralised Planning

It is sometimes now since the decentralised planning process through District Planning Committees came in vogue. During this period of their operation, though not very long, some problems have been identified during the course of the study. We briefly present some of the important ones here.

Participation is the core element in decentralised planning process. In the preparation and consolidation of distinct plan, it was anticipated that local people would actively participate in the planning process which is meant for their own development. The District Planning Committees have thus, been constituted to get this process activated. During the course of the study problems have been reported by the members who affects the participation. In this context it has been pointed that the MPs and MLAs are the members of the DPCs. Their presence in the meetings of the DPC influences the deliberations. The local members shy away from making contribution in the discussion in the meetings which is debating the district plan.

The MPs and MLAs having their own strong political base allegedly try to dominate the proceedings which inhibits the local members either propose any proposal or oppose the proposals submitted by these members. Often the MPs advocate for the inclusion of their own schemes in the district plan which generally takes up the plans for consolidation which has come through the Blocks. The DPCs are generally responsible for consolidating the plans which have been passed and approved by the middle and lower level local government institutions. The pressure from MPs and MLAs creates problem for the local elected members, who try to shy away from such controversies. This therefore, is being considered as a problem in the decentralised planning process.

Related with the problem of active participation of various members in the deliberation of plan preparation, problems connected with ego clashes have also been identified during the course of the field study. As reported in the earlier paragraph, the MPs and MLAs in view of their strong political base and also connections dominate the proceedings in the DPCs whereas as other local elected members get little recognition from the officials and others. This creates a sort of clash of ego amongst the various categories of members in the DPC. This has been considered a problem as it does influence the attitude of the elected members of the DPC.

Problems have been alleged in the plan preparation as well. During the course of the study the members apprised that instead of prescribed process of the plan preparation, there are deviations at times which create problems. Should a scheme or a project proposed, it should be part of the district plan which has not come through the middle and lower planning bodies, has been a subject of criticism by the members. As reported earlier, the MPs and MLAs want their schemes to be part of the district plan which is often not liked by other elected members of the DPC as it has not been approved by appropriate bodies. This results in a problem that affects decentralised planning process.

Lack of co-ordination amongst the members as well as various agencies involved in the decentralised planning has been observed during the course of the study. Due to lack of co-ordination the plan preparation exercise and consolidation gets delayed. Many a times the required information from the concerned organisation does not reach the appropriate body which delays the consolidation process. This therefore, needs to be addressed by the agencies involved in the planning activity at the district level.

Quite a few officials expressed that there is lack of training amongst the members responsible for plan preparation. They alleged that planning requires adequate knowledge and skill. A layman would find it difficult to cope with requirements of such an exercise. The preparation of the plan at the village, the Block and the district levels needs special skills to prepare a realistic plan for the area taking into account the resources available and the requirement for the area. This, they feel, is lacking at different levels and hence creates problem in plan consolidation.

These are in brief some of the problems experienced and identified during the course of the study.

Suggestions

In order to cater to the problems faced by the decentralised planning process and the functioning of the District Planning Committees following suggestions are being presented which may reduce the problem areas and better the decentralised planning.

- A clear demarcation of funds for the rural and urban areas according to the ratio of the population for a balanced planned development.
- Members of Parliament and the Members of Legislative Assembly should not be included in the District Planning Committees in order to encourage local elected members' active participation in the planning and decision-making process at the district level.
- Meetings should regularly be held as prescribed under the law, i.e., three months duration to provide opportunity for debate and discussion on the matter of plan preparation and consolidation.

- A provision of payment of a token honorarium to members attending the DPC meetings could be made to compensate the members for the time they give to the meetings.
- Transparency needs to be maintained in matter of fund allocation and fixation of priority in the district plan to avoid any politicking and nepotism.
- The plan proposals coming through the process of the decentralised planning (i.e., the village, the block and the district) should be accepted instead of proposals submitted by MPs and MLAs exclusive of these bodies.
- A proper co-ordination amongst the various agencies involved in the decentralised planning process should be achieved for efficient and effective planning for development.
- A need-based training should be provided to both—the officials and the non-officials, connected with decentralised planning process. Special courses should be organised for the elected members of the DPCs.
- There should be training of Plan plus software for those connected with plan preparation and consolidation of the plan at different levels.
- Qualified people and experts should be encouraged to join the planning bodies for an improved planning exercise.
- The District Plan prepared and consolidated by the DPC and approved should not be changed to keep the faith of the planning machinery at the district-level intact.
- Provision of prescribing some minimum educational qualification for the members to be elected to the DPC could be considered to have a better functioning of these bodies.

7

Major Findings and Recommendations

The decentralised planning has been on the national agenda from the beginning of our planned effort for development and growth. The progress in this direction, however, remained much below the expectations. One of the factors contributing to the below per performance of decentralised planning process was that required procedures and organisations were not there to match the effort. It was only in the later years that sincere efforts towards decentralised planning were taken up in the country. Ultimately, the constitutional reform measures helped the process of decentralised planning once the District Planning Committees got constituted across the States. We have already dealt with various issues connected the decentralised planning model for development and the role of the DPCs therein. We now propose to briefly present major findings which have come up on the basis of the research study, along with recommendations which may be considered by the authorities concerned to help improve the decentralised planning process.

- The decentralised planning process is a participative process. It is important that elected members take effective part in the planning and decision-making process. It has, however, been found that there are problems in the participative process. Since there are elected local members in the District Planning Committee apart from the MPs and MLAs, who are also there in the DPC due to which some problems have been alleged. In view of this, there has been a suggestion to exclude the MPs and MLAs from the District Planning Committees.

- Meetings of the DPCs are an important formal forum for discussion and debate about the plan allocation as well as fixation of priorities. It has been reported that DPCs meetings have not been regularly concerned which adversely affects the participation and discussion thereof. In view of this, it has been suggested that the meeting of the DPCs should be regularly commenced as prescribed (three months duration).
- The main task assigned to the DPCs is concerned with the consolidation of the district plan. The plans coming through the block after getting formal approval of the requisite authority are then formally received and consolidated by the DPC. However, it has been alleged that the MPs and MLAs get their respective plans included in the district plan over and above the plan received from the lower bodies. This has been objected to by other elected members of the DPC. It is therefore suggested that any plan, project or the scheme of the MPs and MLAs could be included in the district plan after getting due approval from the competent bodies.
- In the decentralised planning process, quite a few agencies are involved apart from the various types of members. Owing to the multiplicity of agencies, after lack of co-ordination has been observed. This lack of co-ordination often delays the planning and consolidating process. Once there is delay in the process, the blame game starts. One agency blames the other for the delay. It is therefore, suggested that responsibility and accountability of the various agencies should be fixed. The delay on the part of the agencies should be identified and action be taken for the same. This would help better the consolidation for effective planning and consolidation.
- Lack of transparency in the planning process has been alleged which causes inefficiency and maladministration. It is, therefore suggested that transparency in every public dealing concerned with the planning at various levels be maintained. It is an important element for good governance and equally important for proper planning.
- Resource allocation is another important activity where problems have been observed. The clash of interest has also come to fore in the discussion dealing the meetings. It is

recommended that funds could be allocated on the basis of rural-urban population ratio. The rural component in a district being generally larger than the urban component, this could be taken as a base for fund allocation.

- Lack of proper understanding and appreciation of planning strategy and skills has been found during the courses of our study. The members generally lack any orientation and skill for plan formulation and consolidation. Due to this lack of training and knowledge the planning process gets otherwise affected by important and irrelevant components. Members often use this forum for lodging their personal complaints rather than providing positive input in the planning process. In view of this, it is recommended that proper need-based training for the elected members may be organised to help better the decentralised planning process.
- To compensate for the lack of training and skill amongst the elected members of the DPC, it recommended that experts could be nominated as members in the DPC. This could help the DPC and other elected members to have a proper and realistic planning exercise.
- The decentralised planning model has been accepted as an appropriate model for development. It is therefore, suggested that this model of development should be continued for future planning and development.
- Some drawbacks have been identified in the composition of the District Planning Committee. Since not much time has passed after they were formally constituted by the States, it is suggested that some more time be given to the existing composition to settle down and take their own corrective measures.
- Since members of the District Planning Committees are generally not educated enough to comprehend the decentralised planning concept and the process involved, the possibility of having some minimum qualification may, by law, be prescribed to get elected in the DPC.

Annexure - I

ICSSR Sponsored Project on
Decentralised Planning Model for Development:
The Role on District Planning Committee

Department of Public Administration,
Lucknow University, Lucknow

QUESTIONNAIRE FOR OFFICIALS

State:________________

District:________________

(A) General Background:

1.	Name of the Respondent	:	....
2.	Name of the Service	:	IAS / PCS / Sub. / Other
3.	Present posting as	:	....
4.	Since when in this job	:	.... (years)
5.	Age	:	....
6.	Educational Qualification	:	Graduate/ Post Graduate / Technical| Any Other
7.	Religion	:	Hindu / Muslim / Sikh / Jain / Buddha / Christian / Any Other
8.	Caste	:	General / SC/ ST / OBC
9.	Family Size	:	....
	Male	:	....
	Female	:	....
10.	Annual Income	:	(Approximate)

11. Promotion received so far in the Service : .... One / Two / Three / None

(B) Planning Process

1. Since how many years you have been associated with planning process? : Less than five years / 5 to 10 years / 10 to 15 years
2. How far you are satisfied with the planning efforts made in your State? : To a large extent / To some extent / Not at all
3. Please name the organisation responsible for preparing a Five Year Plan. : ....
   (a) State : ....
   (b) District : ....
4. How far do you think the planning machinery at different levels is effective :
   (a) State : To a large extent / To some extent / Not at all
   (b) District : To a large extent / To some extent / Not at all
5. How far do you feel that people associated with planning take their job seriously. : To a large extent /To some extent / Not at all
6. Are you aware of the recommendations of the 74th Constitutional Amendment? : Yes / No
7. How far do you think that decentralisation is good for development? : To a large extent / To some extent / Not at all
8. Can you recollect since when Panchayati Raj formally came in existence in your State. : Yes (since) / No
9. Does DRDA exist in your State? : Yes / No

10.	If, yes, who heads DRDA?	:	DM / Chairman Zila Panchayat / Any Other (Specify)

(C) Decentralised Planning

1.	How far do you think that the decentralised planning model has been effective?	:	To a large extent / To some extent / Not at all
2.	Since when your State accepted the decentralised planning model for development?	:	……….. Year
3.	How far do you think that Panchayati Raj System has been successful in your State?	:	To a large extent / To some extent / Not at all
4.	How far do you think 73rd and 74th Constitutional Amendments have made an impact on the planning process in your State?	:	To a large extent /To some extent / Not at all
5.	How far do you think that decentralised planning model is the appropriate model for development in India?	:	To a large extent / To some extent / Not at all
6.	When were the District Planning Committees constituted in your State?	:	……….. Year
7.	Do you think that there was delay in formally constituting the DPC in the State?	:	Yes / No
8.	If yes, what were the main reasons for the delay?	:	………………………………
		:	………………………………
9.	Have the DPC started functioning in your State?	:	Yes / No
10.	In your opinion how many members are there in the DPC?	:	………. (Number)

11.	How far do you think the DPC has been able to perform its tasks in your State satisfactorily.	:	To a large extent / To some extent / Not at all
12.	In how many Five-Year Plan do you think the DPC had a role in your State?	:	One / Two / Three / None
13.	How far do you think the DPC has been able to formulate the Plan in time?	:	To a large extent / To some extent / Not at all
14.	How far do you think the members made serious effort to make a realistic Plan?	:	To a large extent / To some extent / Not at all

15. What were the priorities of the Plan prepared by the DPC?
(Arrange in chronological order)

	Items	*Priority*
(i)	Agriculture	………
(ii)	Small Scale Industry	………
(iii)	Horticulture	………
(iv)	Animal Husbandry	………
(v)	Cash Crops	………
(vi)	Employment Generation	………
(vii)	Education	………
(viii)	Health	………
(ix)	Fisheries	………
(x)	Any Other (Specify)	………

16.	Do you think that the priorities are uniform for the State or they vary from district to district?	:	Uniform / Vary
17.	How far in your opinion the priorities fixed by the DPC are as per the needs of the area?	:	To a large extent / To some extent / Not at all

18. How far in your opinion the strategies for planning in earlier days were effective? : To a large extent / To some extent / Not at all

19. How far do you think comparing the two planning strategies are effective for achieving development? :

    (c) Earlier

    To a large extent / To some extent / Not at all

    (d) Present

    To a large extent / To some extent / Not at all

20. How far do you think the new strategy of decentralised planning has effected change in the perspective? : To a large extent / To some extent / Not at all

(D) Institutional Set up and Networking

1. How far do you agree that there is a large number of institution dealing with decentralised planning? : To a large extent / To some extent / Not at all
2. In your opinion which of the following institutions are involved in decentralised planning? (Tick the answer) : ......
    (i) Govt. Deptts. Concerned ......
    (ii) DRDA ......
    (iii) Panchayati Raj Institution ......
    (iv) District Administration ......
    (v) Any Other ......
3. How far do you think the multiplicity of institutions affects the decentralised planning process? : To a large extent / To some extent / Not at all
4. How far do you think the new institutional network has been able to address the issues adequately? : To a large extent / To some extent / Not at all

5.	How far do you think the involvement of Panchayati Raj institutions has helped the cause of decentralised planning?	:	To a large extent / To some extent / Not at all
6.	How far do you feel satisfied about the co-ordination amongst various institutions engaged in decentralised planning?	:	To a large extent / To some extent / Not at all
7.	How far do you think the institutions involved have taken their job seriously?	:	To a large extent / To some extent / Not at all
8.	How far do you think the institutions have the required skill for the formulation of plans at their levels?	:	To a large extent / To some extent / Not at all
9.	How far do you feel satisfied with infrastructural facility for decentralised planning?	:	To a large extent / To some extent / Not at all
10.	What are your suggestions for making decentralised planning through DPC effective?	:	____________________ ____________________

Annexure - II

ICSSR Sponsored Project on Decentralised Planning Model for Development: The Role of District Planning Committee

Department of Public Administration, Lucknow University, Lucknow

QUESTIONNAIRE FOR NON-OFFICIALS

State:________________________

District:______________________

(A) General Background

1. Name : ....
2. Age : ....
3. Sex (Male / Female) : ....
4. Education : .... Up to Primary / Up to H.S. / Up to Graduate / P.G. and above/ Technical
5. Profession : .... Service / Business / Farmer / Labour
6. Whether member of : Z.P./ K.P./ V.P. / Cooperative / Any Other : ....
7. Family Size : ....

   Male : ....

   Female : ....

8.	Religion	:	.... Hindu / Muslim / Sikh / Jain / Buddha / Christian / Any Other
9.	Caste	:	.... General / SC/ ST / OBC
10.	Monthly Income	:	.... Up to 3,000.00 / up to 10,000.00 / up to 20,000.00/- above 20,000.00

(B) Planning Process

1.	How far are you satisfied with the planning process in your State / District?	:	***(a) State*** — To a large extent / To some extent / Not at all ***(b) District*** — To a large extent / To some extent / Not at all
2.	Have you ever been involved with the planning process?	:	Yes / No
3.	How far do you think planning has been successful?	:	To a large extent / To some extent / Not at all
4.	If not at all, please explain the reasons for not being successful?	:	....
5.	Which are the organisations dealing with planning in your State / District?	:	(a) State: .... (b) District: ....
6.	How far do you think the planning strategies followed so far have been able to address development adequately?	:	To a large extent / To some extent / Not at all
7.	How far do you think planning has been able to tackle poverty and unemployment?	:	To a large extent / To some extent / Not at all
8.	How far do you think Panchayati Raj in your district has been effective in dealing with issues of public?	:	To a large extent / To some extent / Not at all

9.	How far in your opinion the DRDA has been effective in tackling issues of rural development?	:	To a large extent / To some extent / Not at all
10.	Does the DRDA still exist in your district?	:	Yes / No

(C) Decentralised Planning

1.	How far do you think the decentralised planning model is a realistic model for development?	:	To a large extent / To some extent / Not at all
2.	Do you have an idea as to since when the decentralised planning model has been there in the district?	:	.... Year(s)
3.	How far do you think the Panchayati Raj system has been effective in your district?	:	To a large extent / To some extent / Not at all
4.	How far do you think the 73rd and 74th Constitutional Amendments made an impact on the planning process in your district?	:	To a large extent / To some extent / Not at all
5.	How far in your opinion the decentralised planning model is the appropriate model for development?	:	To a large extent / To some extent / Not at all
6.	Since when the District Planning Committee got constituted in your district?	:	.... Year(s)
7.	Do you think there was delay in constituting the DPC in your district?	:	Yes / No
8.	If yes, what were the main reasons for the delay?	:	....
9.	Since when the DPC has started functioning in your district?	:	....

10.	Are you a member of the DPC?	:	Yes / No
11.	If No, are you aware, who are the members of the DPC?	:	Yes / No
12.	How far do you think the DPC has been able to perform their task satisfactorily?	:	To a large extent / To some extent / Not at all
13.	In how many Five Year Plan in your opinion the DPC had a role?	:	One / Two / Three / None
14.	How far do you think the members made a sincere effort to make a realistic plan?	:	To a large extent / To some extent / Not at all
15.	How far do you think the DPC has been able to formulate the plan in time?	:	To a large extent/ To some extent / Not at all
16.	In your opinion what were the priorities of the last Five Year Plan? (Arrange in chronological order)		

Items	*Priority*
(i) Agriculture	....
(ii) Small Scale Industry	....
(iii) Horticulture	....
(iv) Animal Husbandry	....
(v) Cash Crops	....
(vi) Employment Generation	....
(vii) Education	....
(viii) Health	....
(ix) Fisheries	....
(x) Any Other (Specify)	....

17.	Do you think the priorities are uniform for the state or vary from district to district?	:	Uniform / Vary
18.	How far in your opinion the priorities fixed by the DPC	:	To a large extent / To some extent /

	are as per the needs of the area?		Not at all
19.	How far do you think the members of the DPC are knowledgeable enough for the task they have in hand?	:	To a large extent / To some extent / Not at all
20.	How far in your opinion which of the two strategies- earlier and the present one- are effective for achieving development?	:	***Earlier:*** To a large extent / To some extent / Not at all ***Present:*** To a large extent / To some extent / Not at all
21.	How far do you think the new strategies of decentralised planning have effected changes in the perspective?	:	To a large extent / To some extent / Not at all

(D) Institutional Set up and Networking

1.	How far do you agree that there are multiple agencies dealing with decentralised planning?	:	To a large extent / To some extent / Not at all
2.	In your opinion which of the following agencies are involved in decentralised planning?	:	

(Tick the answer)

(i) Govtt. Deptt. Concerned	…………
(ii) DRDA	…………
(iii) Panchayati Raj Institutions	…………
(iv) District Administration	…………
(v) Any Other (Specify)	…………

3.	How far do you think the multiplicity of agencies has affected the decentralised planning process?	:	To a large extent / To some extent / Not at all

4.	How far do you think the new institutional network has been able to address the issues adequately?	:	To a large extent / To some extent / Not at all
5.	How far do you think the involvement of Panchayati Raj institutions has helped the cause of decentralised planning?	:	To a large extent / To some extent / Not at all
6.	How far do you feel that the co-ordination amongst various agencies involved in decentralised planning has been satisfactory?	:	To a large extent / To some extent / Not at all
7.	How far in your opinion the institutions involved have taken their job seriously?	:	To a large extent / To some extent / Not at all
8.	How far do you think the institutions have the required skill for the formulation of the plan at their level?	:	To a large extent / To some extent / Not at all
9.	How far do you feel satisfied with infrastructure facility for decentralised planning?	:	To a large extent / To some extent / Not at all
10.	What are your suggestions for making decentralised planning through the DPC effective?	:	

____

____

____

Index